C-4492   **CAREER EXAMINATION SERIES**

This is your
PASSBOOK for...

Temporary Assistance Specialist I

Test Preparation Study Guide
Questions & Answers

COPYRIGHT NOTICE

This book is SOLELY intended for, is sold ONLY to, and its use is RESTRICTED to individual, bona fide applicants or candidates who qualify by virtue of having seriously filed applications for appropriate license, certificate, professional and/or promotional advancement, higher school matriculation, scholarship, or other legitimate requirements of education and/or governmental authorities.

This book is NOT intended for use, class instruction, tutoring, training, duplication, copying, reprinting, excerption, or adaptation, etc., by:

1) Other publishers
2) Proprietors and/or Instructors of "Coaching" and/or Preparatory Courses
3) Personnel and/or Training Divisions of commercial, industrial, and governmental organizations
4) Schools, colleges, or universities and/or their departments and staffs, including teachers and other personnel
5) Testing Agencies or Bureaus
6) Study groups which seek by the purchase of a single volume to copy and/or duplicate and/or adapt this material for use by the group as a whole without having purchased individual volumes for each of the members of the group
7) Et al.

Such persons would be in violation of appropriate Federal and State statutes.

PROVISION OF LICENSING AGREEMENTS – Recognized educational, commercial, industrial, and governmental institutions and organizations, and others legitimately engaged in educational pursuits, including training, testing, and measurement activities, may address request for a licensing agreement to the copyright owners, who will determine whether, and under what conditions, including fees and charges, the materials in this book may be used them. In other words, a licensing facility exists for the legitimate use of the material in this book on other than an individual basis. However, it is asseverated and affirmed here that the material in this book CANNOT be used without the receipt of the express permission of such a licensing agreement from the Publishers. Inquiries re licensing should be addressed to the company, attention rights and permissions department.

All rights reserved, including the right of reproduction in whole or in part, in any form or by any means, electronic or mechanical, including photocopying, recording, or by any information storage and retrieval system, without permission in writing from the Publisher.

Copyright © 2025 by
National Learning Corporation

212 Michael Drive, Syosset, NY 11791
(516) 921-8888 • www.passbooks.com
E-mail: info@passbooks.com

PASSBOOK® SERIES

THE *PASSBOOK® SERIES* has been created to prepare applicants and candidates for the ultimate academic battlefield – the examination room.

At some time in our lives, each and every one of us may be required to take an examination – for validation, matriculation, admission, qualification, registration, certification, or licensure.

Based on the assumption that every applicant or candidate has met the basic formal educational standards, has taken the required number of courses, and read the necessary texts, the *PASSBOOK® SERIES* furnishes the one special preparation which may assure passing with confidence, instead of failing with insecurity. Examination questions – together with answers – are furnished as the basic vehicle for study so that the mysteries of the examination and its compounding difficulties may be eliminated or diminished by a sure method.

This book is meant to help you pass your examination provided that you qualify and are serious in your objective.

The entire field is reviewed through the huge store of content information which is succinctly presented through a provocative and challenging approach – the question-and-answer method.

A climate of success is established by furnishing the correct answers at the end of each test.

You soon learn to recognize types of questions, forms of questions, and patterns of questioning. You may even begin to anticipate expected outcomes.

You perceive that many questions are repeated or adapted so that you can gain acute insights, which may enable you to score many sure points.

You learn how to confront new questions, or types of questions, and to attack them confidently and work out the correct answers.

You note objectives and emphases, and recognize pitfalls and dangers, so that you may make positive educational adjustments.

Moreover, you are kept fully informed in relation to new concepts, methods, practices, and directions in the field.

You discover that you are actually taking the examination all the time: you are preparing for the examination by "taking" an examination, not by reading extraneous and/or supererogatory textbooks.

In short, this PASSBOOK®, used directedly, should be an important factor in helping you to pass your test.

TEMPORARY ASSISTANCE SPECIALIST I

DUTIES

This is the entry level training class of the series. Under close supervision, incumbents receive on-the-job training and direction, learn the eligibility procedures and regulations for one or more public assistance programs; learn to recognize the need for social services and the appropriate referral process; carry a caseload while receiving close supervision and direction.

As a Temporary Assistance Specialist I, you would provide supporting services or higher level specialists in the development and administration of temporary assistance programs. These services include conducting studies, surveys and reviews; analyzing data; and preparing drafts and abstracts. You would also draft proposals for new regulations, directives and policy guidelines, write letters explaining various aspects of laws, regulation and procedures; and correspond with local social services districts on cost effective ways to meet legal requirements. You would assist senior staff in field work and participate in the development and presentation of training programs in local districts and might supervise subordinate staff.

You would also be expected to gain or to have a thorough understanding of the automated Welfare Management System as it relates to temporary assistance. This involves developing the ability to work with systems staff in enhancing existing programs or developing new ones, defining program requirements which allow the system to manipulate or generate required data; and understanding and analyzing that data. You would also be involved in administering contracts.

KNOWLEDGE AND ABILITIES REQUIRED

Knowledge of: Fundamental aspects of human behavior; general goals of public social service agencies; principles of dealing with the public.

Ability to: Learn interviewing and record keeping techniques and standard office procedures; speak and write effectively; organize work effectively; learn to read, understand and follow complex laws, rules, regulations and policies for at least one public assistance program; follow verbal and written instructions; make accurate arithmetic computations; learn to complete computer input documents; relate to persons of varying social and ethnic backgrounds; learn to perform a high volume of work amid interruptions; perform repetitive work; establish and maintain cooperative working relationships with agency staff and the general public; learn the problems that require referral to social service staff.

1. Current issues and problems in administering assistance programs;
2. Understanding and interpreting written material;
3. Preparing written material;
4. Understanding and interpreting tabular material; and
5. Arithmetical reasoning.

HOW TO TAKE A TEST

I. YOU MUST PASS AN EXAMINATION

A. WHAT EVERY CANDIDATE SHOULD KNOW

Examination applicants often ask us for help in preparing for the written test. What can I study in advance? What kinds of questions will be asked? How will the test be given? How will the papers be graded?

As an applicant for a civil service examination, you may be wondering about some of these things. Our purpose here is to suggest effective methods of advance study and to describe civil service examinations.

Your chances for success on this examination can be increased if you know how to prepare. Those "pre-examination jitters" can be reduced if you know what to expect. You can even experience an adventure in good citizenship if you know why civil service exams are given.

B. WHY ARE CIVIL SERVICE EXAMINATIONS GIVEN?

Civil service examinations are important to you in two ways. As a citizen, you want public jobs filled by employees who know how to do their work. As a job seeker, you want a fair chance to compete for that job on an equal footing with other candidates. The best-known means of accomplishing this two-fold goal is the competitive examination.

Exams are widely publicized throughout the nation. They may be administered for jobs in federal, state, city, municipal, town or village governments or agencies.

Any citizen may apply, with some limitations, such as the age or residence of applicants. Your experience and education may be reviewed to see whether you meet the requirements for the particular examination. When these requirements exist, they are reasonable and applied consistently to all applicants. Thus, a competitive examination may cause you some uneasiness now, but it is your privilege and safeguard.

C. HOW ARE CIVIL SERVICE EXAMS DEVELOPED?

Examinations are carefully written by trained technicians who are specialists in the field known as "psychological measurement," in consultation with recognized authorities in the field of work that the test will cover. These experts recommend the subject matter areas or skills to be tested; only those knowledges or skills important to your success on the job are included. The most reliable books and source materials available are used as references. Together, the experts and technicians judge the difficulty level of the questions.

Test technicians know how to phrase questions so that the problem is clearly stated. Their ethics do not permit "trick" or "catch" questions. Questions may have been tried out on sample groups, or subjected to statistical analysis, to determine their usefulness.

Written tests are often used in combination with performance tests, ratings of training and experience, and oral interviews. All of these measures combine to form the best-known means of finding the right person for the right job.

II. HOW TO PASS THE WRITTEN TEST

A. NATURE OF THE EXAMINATION

To prepare intelligently for civil service examinations, you should know how they differ from school examinations you have taken. In school you were assigned certain definite pages to read or subjects to cover. The examination questions were quite detailed and usually emphasized memory. Civil service exams, on the other hand, try to discover your present ability to perform the duties of a position, plus your potentiality to learn these duties. In other words, a civil service exam attempts to predict how successful you will be. Questions cover such a broad area that they cannot be as minute and detailed as school exam questions.

In the public service similar kinds of work, or positions, are grouped together in one "class." This process is known as *position-classification*. All the positions in a class are paid according to the salary range for that class. One class title covers all of these positions, and they are all tested by the same examination.

B. FOUR BASIC STEPS

1) Study the announcement

How, then, can you know what subjects to study? Our best answer is: "Learn as much as possible about the class of positions for which you've applied." The exam will test the knowledge, skills and abilities needed to do the work.

Your most valuable source of information about the position you want is the official exam announcement. This announcement lists the training and experience qualifications. Check these standards and apply only if you come reasonably close to meeting them.

The brief description of the position in the examination announcement offers some clues to the subjects which will be tested. Think about the job itself. Review the duties in your mind. Can you perform them, or are there some in which you are rusty? Fill in the blank spots in your preparation.

Many jurisdictions preview the written test in the exam announcement by including a section called "Knowledge and Abilities Required," "Scope of the Examination," or some similar heading. Here you will find out specifically what fields will be tested.

2) Review your own background

Once you learn in general what the position is all about, and what you need to know to do the work, ask yourself which subjects you already know fairly well and which need improvement. You may wonder whether to concentrate on improving your strong areas or on building some background in your fields of weakness. When the announcement has specified "some knowledge" or "considerable knowledge," or has used adjectives like "beginning principles of…" or "advanced … methods," you can get a clue as to the number and difficulty of questions to be asked in any given field. More questions, and hence broader coverage, would be included for those subjects which are more important in the work. Now weigh your strengths and weaknesses against the job requirements and prepare accordingly.

3) Determine the level of the position

Another way to tell how intensively you should prepare is to understand the level of the job for which you are applying. Is it the entering level? In other words, is this the position in which beginners in a field of work are hired? Or is it an intermediate or advanced level? Sometimes this is indicated by such words as "Junior" or "Senior" in the class title. Other jurisdictions use Roman numerals to designate the level – Clerk I, Clerk II, for example. The word "Supervisor" sometimes appears in the title. If the level is not indicated by the title, check the description of duties. Will you be working under very close supervision, or will you have responsibility for independent decisions in this work?

4) Choose appropriate study materials

Now that you know the subjects to be examined and the relative amount of each subject to be covered, you can choose suitable study materials. For beginning level jobs, or even advanced ones, if you have a pronounced weakness in some aspect of your training, read a modern, standard textbook in that field. Be sure it is up to date and has general coverage. Such books are normally available at your library, and the librarian will be glad to help you locate one. For entry-level positions, questions of appropriate difficulty are chosen – neither highly advanced questions, nor those too simple. Such questions require careful thought but not advanced training.

If the position for which you are applying is technical or advanced, you will read more advanced, specialized material. If you are already familiar with the basic principles of your field, elementary textbooks would waste your time. Concentrate on advanced textbooks and technical periodicals. Think through the concepts and review difficult problems in your field.

These are all general sources. You can get more ideas on your own initiative, following these leads. For example, training manuals and publications of the government agency which employs workers in your field can be useful, particularly for technical and professional positions. A letter or visit to the government department involved may result in more specific study suggestions, and certainly will provide you with a more definite idea of the exact nature of the position you are seeking.

III. KINDS OF TESTS

Tests are used for purposes other than measuring knowledge and ability to perform specified duties. For some positions, it is equally important to test ability to make adjustments to new situations or to profit from training. In others, basic mental abilities not dependent on information are essential. Questions which test these things may not appear as pertinent to the duties of the position as those which test for knowledge and information. Yet they are often highly important parts of a fair examination. For very general questions, it is almost impossible to help you direct your study efforts. What we can do is to point out some of the more common of these general abilities needed in public service positions and describe some typical questions.

1) General information

Broad, general information has been found useful for predicting job success in some kinds of work. This is tested in a variety of ways, from vocabulary lists to questions about current events. Basic background in some field of work, such as sociology or economics, may be sampled in a group of questions. Often these are principles which have become familiar to most persons through exposure rather than through formal training. It is difficult to advise you how to study for these questions; being alert to the world around you is our best suggestion.

2) Verbal ability

An example of an ability needed in many positions is verbal or language ability. Verbal ability is, in brief, the ability to use and understand words. Vocabulary and grammar tests are typical measures of this ability. Reading comprehension or paragraph interpretation questions are common in many kinds of civil service tests. You are given a paragraph of written material and asked to find its central meaning.

3) Numerical ability

Number skills can be tested by the familiar arithmetic problem, by checking paired lists of numbers to see which are alike and which are different, or by interpreting charts and graphs. In the latter test, a graph may be printed in the test booklet which you are asked to use as the basis for answering questions.

4) Observation

A popular test for law-enforcement positions is the observation test. A picture is shown to you for several minutes, then taken away. Questions about the picture test your ability to observe both details and larger elements.

5) Following directions

In many positions in the public service, the employee must be able to carry out written instructions dependably and accurately. You may be given a chart with several columns, each column listing a variety of information. The questions require you to carry out directions involving the information given in the chart.

6) Skills and aptitudes

Performance tests effectively measure some manual skills and aptitudes. When the skill is one in which you are trained, such as typing or shorthand, you can practice. These tests are often very much like those given in business school or high school courses. For many of the other skills and aptitudes, however, no short-time preparation can be made. Skills and abilities natural to you or that you have developed throughout your lifetime are being tested.

Many of the general questions just described provide all the data needed to answer the questions and ask you to use your reasoning ability to find the answers. Your best preparation for these tests, as well as for tests of facts and ideas, is to be at your physical and mental best. You, no doubt, have your own methods of getting into an exam-taking mood and keeping "in shape." The next section lists some ideas on this subject.

IV. KINDS OF QUESTIONS

Only rarely is the "essay" question, which you answer in narrative form, used in civil service tests. Civil service tests are usually of the short-answer type. Full instructions for answering these questions will be given to you at the examination. But in case this is your first experience with short-answer questions and separate answer sheets, here is what you need to know:

1) Multiple-choice Questions

Most popular of the short-answer questions is the "multiple choice" or "best answer" question. It can be used, for example, to test for factual knowledge, ability to solve problems or judgment in meeting situations found at work.

A multiple-choice question is normally one of three types—
- It can begin with an incomplete statement followed by several possible endings. You are to find the one ending which *best* completes the statement, although some of the others may not be entirely wrong.
- It can also be a complete statement in the form of a question which is answered by choosing one of the statements listed.

- It can be in the form of a problem – again you select the best answer.

Here is an example of a multiple-choice question with a discussion which should give you some clues as to the method for choosing the right answer:

When an employee has a complaint about his assignment, the action which will *best* help him overcome his difficulty is to
- A. discuss his difficulty with his coworkers
- B. take the problem to the head of the organization
- C. take the problem to the person who gave him the assignment
- D. say nothing to anyone about his complaint

In answering this question, you should study each of the choices to find which is best. Consider choice "A" – Certainly an employee may discuss his complaint with fellow employees, but no change or improvement can result, and the complaint remains unresolved. Choice "B" is a poor choice since the head of the organization probably does not know what assignment you have been given, and taking your problem to him is known as "going over the head" of the supervisor. The supervisor, or person who made the assignment, is the person who can clarify it or correct any injustice. Choice "C" is, therefore, correct. To say nothing, as in choice "D," is unwise. Supervisors have and interest in knowing the problems employees are facing, and the employee is seeking a solution to his problem.

2) True/False Questions

The "true/false" or "right/wrong" form of question is sometimes used. Here a complete statement is given. Your job is to decide whether the statement is right or wrong.

SAMPLE: A roaming cell-phone call to a nearby city costs less than a non-roaming call to a distant city.

This statement is wrong, or false, since roaming calls are more expensive.

This is not a complete list of all possible question forms, although most of the others are variations of these common types. You will always get complete directions for answering questions. Be sure you understand *how* to mark your answers – ask questions until you do.

V. RECORDING YOUR ANSWERS

Computer terminals are used more and more today for many different kinds of exams.

For an examination with very few applicants, you may be told to record your answers in the test booklet itself. Separate answer sheets are much more common. If this separate answer sheet is to be scored by machine – and this is often the case – it is highly important that you mark your answers correctly in order to get credit.

An electronic scoring machine is often used in civil service offices because of the speed with which papers can be scored. Machine-scored answer sheets must be marked with a pencil, which will be given to you. This pencil has a high graphite content which responds to the electronic scoring machine. As a matter of fact, stray dots may register as answers, so do not let your pencil rest on the answer sheet while you are pondering the correct answer. Also, if your pencil lead breaks or is otherwise defective, ask for another.

Since the answer sheet will be dropped in a slot in the scoring machine, be careful not to bend the corners or get the paper crumpled.

The answer sheet normally has five vertical columns of numbers, with 30 numbers to a column. These numbers correspond to the question numbers in your test booklet. After each number, going across the page are four or five pairs of dotted lines. These short dotted lines have small letters or numbers above them. The first two pairs may also have a "T" or "F" above the letters. This indicates that the first two pairs only are to be used if the questions are of the true-false type. If the questions are multiple choice, disregard the "T" and "F" and pay attention only to the small letters or numbers.

Answer your questions in the manner of the sample that follows:

32. The largest city in the United States is
    A. Washington, D.C.
    B. New York City
    C. Chicago
    D. Detroit
    E. San Francisco

1) Choose the answer you think is best. (New York City is the largest, so "B" is correct.)
2) Find the row of dotted lines numbered the same as the question you are answering. (Find row number 32)
3) Find the pair of dotted lines corresponding to the answer. (Find the pair of lines under the mark "B.")
4) Make a solid black mark between the dotted lines.

VI. BEFORE THE TEST

Common sense will help you find procedures to follow to get ready for an examination. Too many of us, however, overlook these sensible measures. Indeed, nervousness and fatigue have been found to be the most serious reasons why applicants fail to do their best on civil service tests. Here is a list of reminders:

- Begin your preparation early – Don't wait until the last minute to go scurrying around for books and materials or to find out what the position is all about.
- Prepare continuously – An hour a night for a week is better than an all-night cram session. This has been definitely established. What is more, a night a week for a month will return better dividends than crowding your study into a shorter period of time.
- Locate the place of the exam – You have been sent a notice telling you when and where to report for the examination. If the location is in a different town or otherwise unfamiliar to you, it would be well to inquire the best route and learn something about the building.
- Relax the night before the test – Allow your mind to rest. Do not study at all that night. Plan some mild recreation or diversion; then go to bed early and get a good night's sleep.
- Get up early enough to make a leisurely trip to the place for the test – This way unforeseen events, traffic snarls, unfamiliar buildings, etc. will not upset you.
- Dress comfortably – A written test is not a fashion show. You will be known by number and not by name, so wear something comfortable.

- Leave excess paraphernalia at home – Shopping bags and odd bundles will get in your way. You need bring only the items mentioned in the official notice you received; usually everything you need is provided. Do not bring reference books to the exam. They will only confuse those last minutes and be taken away from you when in the test room.
- Arrive somewhat ahead of time – If because of transportation schedules you must get there very early, bring a newspaper or magazine to take your mind off yourself while waiting.
- Locate the examination room – When you have found the proper room, you will be directed to the seat or part of the room where you will sit. Sometimes you are given a sheet of instructions to read while you are waiting. Do not fill out any forms until you are told to do so; just read them and be prepared.
- Relax and prepare to listen to the instructions
- If you have any physical problem that may keep you from doing your best, be sure to tell the test administrator. If you are sick or in poor health, you really cannot do your best on the exam. You can come back and take the test some other time.

VII. AT THE TEST

The day of the test is here and you have the test booklet in your hand. The temptation to get going is very strong. Caution! There is more to success than knowing the right answers. You must know how to identify your papers and understand variations in the type of short-answer question used in this particular examination. Follow these suggestions for maximum results from your efforts:

1) Cooperate with the monitor

The test administrator has a duty to create a situation in which you can be as much at ease as possible. He will give instructions, tell you when to begin, check to see that you are marking your answer sheet correctly, and so on. He is not there to guard you, although he will see that your competitors do not take unfair advantage. He wants to help you do your best.

2) Listen to all instructions

Don't jump the gun! Wait until you understand all directions. In most civil service tests you get more time than you need to answer the questions. So don't be in a hurry. Read each word of instructions until you clearly understand the meaning. Study the examples, listen to all announcements and follow directions. Ask questions if you do not understand what to do.

3) Identify your papers

Civil service exams are usually identified by number only. You will be assigned a number; you must not put your name on your test papers. Be sure to copy your number correctly. Since more than one exam may be given, copy your exact examination title.

4) Plan your time

Unless you are told that a test is a "speed" or "rate of work" test, speed itself is usually not important. Time enough to answer all the questions will be provided, but this does not mean that you have all day. An overall time limit has been set. Divide the total time (in minutes) by the number of questions to determine the approximate time you have for each question.

5) Do not linger over difficult questions

If you come across a difficult question, mark it with a paper clip (useful to have along) and come back to it when you have been through the booklet. One caution if you do this – be sure to skip a number on your answer sheet as well. Check often to be sure that you have not lost your place and that you are marking in the row numbered the same as the question you are answering.

6) Read the questions

Be sure you know what the question asks! Many capable people are unsuccessful because they failed to *read* the questions correctly.

7) Answer all questions

Unless you have been instructed that a penalty will be deducted for incorrect answers, it is better to guess than to omit a question.

8) Speed tests

It is often better NOT to guess on speed tests. It has been found that on timed tests people are tempted to spend the last few seconds before time is called in marking answers at random – without even reading them – in the hope of picking up a few extra points. To discourage this practice, the instructions may warn you that your score will be "corrected" for guessing. That is, a penalty will be applied. The incorrect answers will be deducted from the correct ones, or some other penalty formula will be used.

9) Review your answers

If you finish before time is called, go back to the questions you guessed or omitted to give them further thought. Review other answers if you have time.

10) Return your test materials

If you are ready to leave before others have finished or time is called, take ALL your materials to the monitor and leave quietly. Never take any test material with you. The monitor can discover whose papers are not complete, and taking a test booklet may be grounds for disqualification.

VIII. EXAMINATION TECHNIQUES

1) Read the general instructions carefully. These are usually printed on the first page of the exam booklet. As a rule, these instructions refer to the timing of the examination; the fact that you should not start work until the signal and must stop work at a signal, etc. If there are any *special* instructions, such as a choice of questions to be answered, make sure that you note this instruction carefully.

2) When you are ready to start work on the examination, that is as soon as the signal has been given, read the instructions to each question booklet, underline any key words or phrases, such as *least, best, outline, describe* and the like. In this way you will tend to answer as requested rather than discover on reviewing your paper that you *listed without describing*, that you selected the *worst* choice rather than the *best* choice, etc.

3) If the examination is of the objective or multiple-choice type – that is, each question will also give a series of possible answers: A, B, C or D, and you are called upon to select the best answer and write the letter next to that answer on your answer paper – it is advisable to start answering each question in turn. There may be anywhere from 50 to 100 such questions in the three or four hours allotted and you can see how much time would be taken if you read through all the questions before beginning to answer any. Furthermore, if you come across a question or group of questions which you know would be difficult to answer, it would undoubtedly affect your handling of all the other questions.

4) If the examination is of the essay type and contains but a few questions, it is a moot point as to whether you should read all the questions before starting to answer any one. Of course, if you are given a choice – say five out of seven and the like – then it is essential to read all the questions so you can eliminate the two that are most difficult. If, however, you are asked to answer all the questions, there may be danger in trying to answer the easiest one first because you may find that you will spend too much time on it. The best technique is to answer the first question, then proceed to the second, etc.

5) Time your answers. Before the exam begins, write down the time it started, then add the time allowed for the examination and write down the time it must be completed, then divide the time available somewhat as follows:
    - If 3-1/2 hours are allowed, that would be 210 minutes. If you have 80 objective-type questions, that would be an average of 2-1/2 minutes per question. Allow yourself no more than 2 minutes per question, or a total of 160 minutes, which will permit about 50 minutes to review.
    - If for the time allotment of 210 minutes there are 7 essay questions to answer, that would average about 30 minutes a question. Give yourself only 25 minutes per question so that you have about 35 minutes to review.

6) The most important instruction is to *read each question* and make sure you know what is wanted. The second most important instruction is to *time yourself properly* so that you answer every question. The third most important instruction is to *answer every question*. Guess if you have to but include something for each question. Remember that you will receive no credit for a blank and will probably receive some credit if you write something in answer to an essay question. If you guess a letter – say "B" for a multiple-choice question – you may have guessed right. If you leave a blank as an answer to a multiple-choice question, the examiners may respect your feelings but it will not add a point to your score. Some exams may penalize you for wrong answers, so in such cases *only*, you may not want to guess unless you have some basis for your answer.

7) Suggestions
    a. Objective-type questions
        1. Examine the question booklet for proper sequence of pages and questions
        2. Read all instructions carefully
        3. Skip any question which seems too difficult; return to it after all other questions have been answered
        4. Apportion your time properly; do not spend too much time on any single question or group of questions

5. Note and underline key words – *all, most, fewest, least, best, worst, same, opposite*, etc.
6. Pay particular attention to negatives
7. Note unusual option, e.g., unduly long, short, complex, different or similar in content to the body of the question
8. Observe the use of "hedging" words – *probably, may, most likely,* etc.
9. Make sure that your answer is put next to the same number as the question
10. Do not second-guess unless you have good reason to believe the second answer is definitely more correct
11. Cross out original answer if you decide another answer is more accurate; do not erase until you are ready to hand your paper in
12. Answer all questions; guess unless instructed otherwise
13. Leave time for review

b. Essay questions
1. Read each question carefully
2. Determine exactly what is wanted. Underline key words or phrases.
3. Decide on outline or paragraph answer
4. Include many different points and elements unless asked to develop any one or two points or elements
5. Show impartiality by giving pros and cons unless directed to select one side only
6. Make and write down any assumptions you find necessary to answer the questions
7. Watch your English, grammar, punctuation and choice of words
8. Time your answers; don't crowd material

8) Answering the essay question

Most essay questions can be answered by framing the specific response around several key words or ideas. Here are a few such key words or ideas:

M's: manpower, materials, methods, money, management
P's: purpose, program, policy, plan, procedure, practice, problems, pitfalls, personnel, public relations

a. Six basic steps in handling problems:
1. Preliminary plan and background development
2. Collect information, data and facts
3. Analyze and interpret information, data and facts
4. Analyze and develop solutions as well as make recommendations
5. Prepare report and sell recommendations
6. Install recommendations and follow up effectiveness

b. Pitfalls to avoid
1. *Taking things for granted* – A statement of the situation does not necessarily imply that each of the elements is necessarily true; for example, a complaint may be invalid and biased so that all that can be taken for granted is that a complaint has been registered

2. *Considering only one side of a situation* – Wherever possible, indicate several alternatives and then point out the reasons you selected the best one
3. *Failing to indicate follow up* – Whenever your answer indicates action on your part, make certain that you will take proper follow-up action to see how successful your recommendations, procedures or actions turn out to be
4. *Taking too long in answering any single question* – Remember to time your answers properly

IX. AFTER THE TEST

Scoring procedures differ in detail among civil service jurisdictions although the general principles are the same. Whether the papers are hand-scored or graded by machine we have described, they are nearly always graded by number. That is, the person who marks the paper knows only the number – never the name – of the applicant. Not until all the papers have been graded will they be matched with names. If other tests, such as training and experience or oral interview ratings have been given, scores will be combined. Different parts of the examination usually have different weights. For example, the written test might count 60 percent of the final grade, and a rating of training and experience 40 percent. In many jurisdictions, veterans will have a certain number of points added to their grades.

After the final grade has been determined, the names are placed in grade order and an eligible list is established. There are various methods for resolving ties between those who get the same final grade – probably the most common is to place first the name of the person whose application was received first. Job offers are made from the eligible list in the order the names appear on it. You will be notified of your grade and your rank as soon as all these computations have been made. This will be done as rapidly as possible.

People who are found to meet the requirements in the announcement are called "eligibles." Their names are put on a list of eligible candidates. An eligible's chances of getting a job depend on how high he stands on this list and how fast agencies are filling jobs from the list.

When a job is to be filled from a list of eligibles, the agency asks for the names of people on the list of eligibles for that job. When the civil service commission receives this request, it sends to the agency the names of the three people highest on this list. Or, if the job to be filled has specialized requirements, the office sends the agency the names of the top three persons who meet these requirements from the general list.

The appointing officer makes a choice from among the three people whose names were sent to him. If the selected person accepts the appointment, the names of the others are put back on the list to be considered for future openings.

That is the rule in hiring from all kinds of eligible lists, whether they are for typist, carpenter, chemist, or something else. For every vacancy, the appointing officer has his choice of any one of the top three eligibles on the list. This explains why the person whose name is on top of the list sometimes does not get an appointment when some of the persons lower on the list do. If the appointing officer chooses the second or third eligible, the No. 1 eligible does not get a job at once, but stays on the list until he is appointed or the list is terminated.

X. HOW TO PASS THE INTERVIEW TEST

The examination for which you applied requires an oral interview test. You have already taken the written test and you are now being called for the interview test – the final part of the formal examination.

You may think that it is not possible to prepare for an interview test and that there are no procedures to follow during an interview. Our purpose is to point out some things you can do in advance that will help you and some good rules to follow and pitfalls to avoid while you are being interviewed.

What is an interview supposed to test?

The written examination is designed to test the technical knowledge and competence of the candidate; the oral is designed to evaluate intangible qualities, not readily measured otherwise, and to establish a list showing the relative fitness of each candidate – as measured against his competitors – for the position sought. Scoring is not on the basis of "right" and "wrong," but on a sliding scale of values ranging from "not passable" to "outstanding." As a matter of fact, it is possible to achieve a relatively low score without a single "incorrect" answer because of evident weakness in the qualities being measured.

Occasionally, an examination may consist entirely of an oral test – either an individual or a group oral. In such cases, information is sought concerning the technical knowledges and abilities of the candidate, since there has been no written examination for this purpose. More commonly, however, an oral test is used to supplement a written examination.

Who conducts interviews?

The composition of oral boards varies among different jurisdictions. In nearly all, a representative of the personnel department serves as chairman. One of the members of the board may be a representative of the department in which the candidate would work. In some cases, "outside experts" are used, and, frequently, a businessman or some other representative of the general public is asked to serve. Labor and management or other special groups may be represented. The aim is to secure the services of experts in the appropriate field.

However the board is composed, it is a good idea (and not at all improper or unethical) to ascertain in advance of the interview who the members are and what groups they represent. When you are introduced to them, you will have some idea of their backgrounds and interests, and at least you will not stutter and stammer over their names.

What should be done before the interview?

While knowledge about the board members is useful and takes some of the surprise element out of the interview, there is other preparation which is more substantive. It *is* possible to prepare for an oral interview – in several ways:

1) Keep a copy of your application and review it carefully before the interview

This may be the only document before the oral board, and the starting point of the interview. Know what education and experience you have listed there, and the sequence and dates of all of it. Sometimes the board will ask you to review the highlights of your experience for them; you should not have to hem and haw doing it.

2) Study the class specification and the examination announcement

Usually, the oral board has one or both of these to guide them. The qualities, characteristics or knowledges required by the position sought are stated in these documents. They offer valuable clues as to the nature of the oral interview. For example, if the job involves supervisory responsibilities, the announcement will usually indicate that knowledge of modern supervisory methods and the qualifications of the candidate as a supervisor will be tested. If so, you can expect such questions, frequently in the form of a hypothetical situation which you are expected to solve. NEVER go into an oral without knowledge of the duties and responsibilities of the job you seek.

3) Think through each qualification required

Try to visualize the kind of questions you would ask if you were a board member. How well could you answer them? Try especially to appraise your own knowledge and background in each area, *measured against the job sought*, and identify any areas in which you are weak. Be critical and realistic – do not flatter yourself.

4) Do some general reading in areas in which you feel you may be weak

For example, if the job involves supervision and your past experience has NOT, some general reading in supervisory methods and practices, particularly in the field of human relations, might be useful. Do NOT study agency procedures or detailed manuals. The oral board will be testing your understanding and capacity, not your memory.

5) Get a good night's sleep and watch your general health and mental attitude

You will want a clear head at the interview. Take care of a cold or any other minor ailment, and of course, no hangovers.

What should be done on the day of the interview?

Now comes the day of the interview itself. Give yourself plenty of time to get there. Plan to arrive somewhat ahead of the scheduled time, particularly if your appointment is in the fore part of the day. If a previous candidate fails to appear, the board might be ready for you a bit early. By early afternoon an oral board is almost invariably behind schedule if there are many candidates, and you may have to wait. Take along a book or magazine to read, or your application to review, but leave any extraneous material in the waiting room when you go in for your interview. In any event, relax and compose yourself.

The matter of dress is important. The board is forming impressions about you – from your experience, your manners, your attitude, and your appearance. Give your personal appearance careful attention. Dress your best, but not your flashiest. Choose conservative, appropriate clothing, and be sure it is immaculate. This is a business interview, and your appearance should indicate that you regard it as such. Besides, being well groomed and properly dressed will help boost your confidence.

Sooner or later, someone will call your name and escort you into the interview room. *This is it*. From here on you are on your own. It is too late for any more preparation. But remember, you asked for this opportunity to prove your fitness, and you are here because your request was granted.

What happens when you go in?

The usual sequence of events will be as follows: The clerk (who is often the board stenographer) will introduce you to the chairman of the oral board, who will introduce you to the other members of the board. Acknowledge the introductions before you sit down. Do not be surprised if you find a microphone facing you or a stenotypist sitting by. Oral interviews are usually recorded in the event of an appeal or other review.

Usually the chairman of the board will open the interview by reviewing the highlights of your education and work experience from your application – primarily for the benefit of the other members of the board, as well as to get the material into the record. Do not interrupt or comment unless there is an error or significant misinterpretation; if that is the case, do not hesitate. But do not quibble about insignificant matters. Also, he will usually ask you some question about your education, experience or your present job – partly to get you to start talking and to establish the interviewing "rapport." He may start the actual questioning, or turn it over to one of the other members. Frequently, each member undertakes the questioning on a particular area, one in which he is perhaps most competent, so you can expect each member to participate in the examination. Because time is limited, you may also expect some rather abrupt switches in the direction the questioning takes, so do not be upset by it. Normally, a board member will not pursue a single line of questioning unless he discovers a particular strength or weakness.

After each member has participated, the chairman will usually ask whether any member has any further questions, then will ask you if you have anything you wish to add. Unless you are expecting this question, it may floor you. Worse, it may start you off on an extended, extemporaneous speech. The board is not usually seeking more information. The question is principally to offer you a last opportunity to present further qualifications or to indicate that you have nothing to add. So, if you feel that a significant qualification or characteristic has been overlooked, it is proper to point it out in a sentence or so. Do not compliment the board on the thoroughness of their examination – they have been sketchy, and you know it. If you wish, merely say, "No thank you, I have nothing further to add." This is a point where you can "talk yourself out" of a good impression or fail to present an important bit of information. Remember, *you close the interview yourself*.

The chairman will then say, "That is all, Mr. _____, thank you." Do not be startled; the interview is over, and quicker than you think. Thank him, gather your belongings and take your leave. Save your sigh of relief for the other side of the door.

How to put your best foot forward

Throughout this entire process, you may feel that the board individually and collectively is trying to pierce your defenses, seek out your hidden weaknesses and embarrass and confuse you. Actually, this is not true. They are obliged to make an appraisal of your qualifications for the job you are seeking, and they want to see you in your best light. Remember, they must interview all candidates and a non-cooperative candidate may become a failure in spite of their best efforts to bring out his qualifications. Here are 15 suggestions that will help you:

1) Be natural – Keep your attitude confident, not cocky

If you are not confident that you can do the job, do not expect the board to be. Do not apologize for your weaknesses, try to bring out your strong points. The board is interested in a positive, not negative, presentation. Cockiness will antagonize any board member and make him wonder if you are covering up a weakness by a false show of strength.

2) Get comfortable, but don't lounge or sprawl

Sit erectly but not stiffly. A careless posture may lead the board to conclude that you are careless in other things, or at least that you are not impressed by the importance of the occasion. Either conclusion is natural, even if incorrect. Do not fuss with your clothing, a pencil or an ashtray. Your hands may occasionally be useful to emphasize a point; do not let them become a point of distraction.

3) Do not wisecrack or make small talk

This is a serious situation, and your attitude should show that you consider it as such. Further, the time of the board is limited – they do not want to waste it, and neither should you.

4) Do not exaggerate your experience or abilities

In the first place, from information in the application or other interviews and sources, the board may know more about you than you think. Secondly, you probably will not get away with it. An experienced board is rather adept at spotting such a situation, so do not take the chance.

5) If you know a board member, do not make a point of it, yet do not hide it

Certainly you are not fooling him, and probably not the other members of the board. Do not try to take advantage of your acquaintanceship – it will probably do you little good.

6) Do not dominate the interview

Let the board do that. They will give you the clues – do not assume that you have to do all the talking. Realize that the board has a number of questions to ask you, and do not try to take up all the interview time by showing off your extensive knowledge of the answer to the first one.

7) Be attentive

You only have 20 minutes or so, and you should keep your attention at its sharpest throughout. When a member is addressing a problem or question to you, give him your undivided attention. Address your reply principally to him, but do not exclude the other board members.

8) Do not interrupt

A board member may be stating a problem for you to analyze. He will ask you a question when the time comes. Let him state the problem, and wait for the question.

9) Make sure you understand the question

Do not try to answer until you are sure what the question is. If it is not clear, restate it in your own words or ask the board member to clarify it for you. However, do not haggle about minor elements.

10) Reply promptly but not hastily

A common entry on oral board rating sheets is "candidate responded readily," or "candidate hesitated in replies." Respond as promptly and quickly as you can, but do not jump to a hasty, ill-considered answer.

11) Do not be peremptory in your answers

A brief answer is proper – but do not fire your answer back. That is a losing game from your point of view. The board member can probably ask questions much faster than you can answer them.

12) Do not try to create the answer you think the board member wants

He is interested in what kind of mind you have and how it works – not in playing games. Furthermore, he can usually spot this practice and will actually grade you down on it.

13) Do not switch sides in your reply merely to agree with a board member

Frequently, a member will take a contrary position merely to draw you out and to see if you are willing and able to defend your point of view. Do not start a debate, yet do not surrender a good position. If a position is worth taking, it is worth defending.

14) Do not be afraid to admit an error in judgment if you are shown to be wrong

The board knows that you are forced to reply without any opportunity for careful consideration. Your answer may be demonstrably wrong. If so, admit it and get on with the interview.

15) Do not dwell at length on your present job

The opening question may relate to your present assignment. Answer the question but do not go into an extended discussion. You are being examined for a *new* job, not your present one. As a matter of fact, try to phrase ALL your answers in terms of the job for which you are being examined.

Basis of Rating

Probably you will forget most of these "do's" and "don'ts" when you walk into the oral interview room. Even remembering them all will not ensure you a passing grade. Perhaps you did not have the qualifications in the first place. But remembering them will help you to put your best foot forward, without treading on the toes of the board members.

Rumor and popular opinion to the contrary notwithstanding, an oral board wants you to make the best appearance possible. They know you are under pressure – but they also want to see how you respond to it as a guide to what your reaction would be under the pressures of the job you seek. They will be influenced by the degree of poise you display, the personal traits you show and the manner in which you respond.

ABOUT THIS BOOK

This book contains tests divided into Examination Sections. Go through each test, answering every question in the margin. We have also attached a sample answer sheet at the back of the book that can be removed and used. At the end of each test look at the answer key and check your answers. On the ones you got wrong, look at the right answer choice and learn. Do not fill in the answers first. Do not memorize the questions and answers, but understand the answer and principles involved. On your test, the questions will likely be different from the samples. Questions are changed and new ones added. If you understand these past questions you should have success with any changes that arise. Tests may consist of several types of questions. We have additional books on each subject should more study be advisable or necessary for you. Finally, the more you study, the better prepared you will be. This book is intended to be the last thing you study before you walk into the examination room. Prior study of relevant texts is also recommended. NLC publishes some of these in our Fundamental Series. Knowledge and good sense are important factors in passing your exam. Good luck also helps. So now study this Passbook, absorb the material contained within and take that knowledge into the examination. Then do your best to pass that exam.

EXAMINATION SECTION

EXAMINATION SECTION
TEST 1

DIRECTIONS: Each question or incomplete statement is followed by several suggested answers or completions. Select the one the BEST answers the question or completes the statement. *PRINT THE LETTER OF THE CORRECT ANSWER IN THE SPACE AT THE RIGHT.*

1. Assuming the absence of any other disqualifying factor, which of the following would be eligible for Transitional Child Care?
    I. Vernon, age 32, a single father of a 12-year-old daughter, who has just been hired at a new job and previously received Family Assistance. The state income standard is $1000 a month; his income at the new job will be $1800 a month.
    II. Carol, age 45, a single mother of two children, ages 2 and 6. She has not received public assistance in more than a year, but recent pay cuts have dropped her below the poverty level.
    III. Robert, age 48, a single father of a 14-year-old daughter, who received family assistance until being hired to work as a clerk at a law firm. The state income standard is $1000 a month; his income at the new job will be $1500 a month.

    A. I only
    B. I and II
    C. II and III
    D. I, II and III

2. A family's standard of need for their area is $419 per month. To pass the gross income test and therefore qualify for income disregards, the family's gross monthly income cannot exceed $ _____.

    A. 419.00
    B. 628.50
    C. 775.15
    D. 838.00

3. The Welfare Reform Act of 1997 mandates that all applicants or recipients aged _____ or over must submit to screening for the presence of an alcohol or substance abuse problem.

    A. 13
    B. 15
    C. 18
    D. 21

4. The "Work First" goal of the Welfare Reform Act of 1997 is typically set aside when the client
    I. is a victim of domestic violence and working or participating in work activities may place him/her in danger
    II. is the single parent of one or more children under the age of 3
    III. has a significant disability and is applying for federal SSI

    A. I only   B. I and III   C. II and III   D. I, II and III

5. A woman who is pregnant is eligible for Family Assistance

   A. as soon as the pregnancy is medically verified
   B. after the first trimester
   C. after the second trimester
   D. as soon as the child is born

6. A Temporary Assistance recipient, a single mother, has been sanctioned for not complying with the alcohol/illegal substance screening requirements of her benefit agreement. After official sanction, the consequence for this recipient is a

   A. $50 deduction from monthly cash assistance payments
   B. 25% reduction in her monthly cash assistance payment
   C. total disqualification from benefits
   D. total disqualification from benefits and criminal prosecution, it can be determined that the client is using an illegal substance

7. Generally, minors who are at least _____ years old can have a Temporary Assistance case opened in their own name.

   A. 13   B. 16   C. 17   D. 18

8. Pregnant women are exempted from work requirements under workfare programs

   A. throughout their entire pregnancy
   B. after the first trimester
   C. after the second trimester
   D. after the eighth month

9. For a single parent with a dependent child younger than 6, the minimum number of weekly work hours required for Temporary Assistance benefits would be

   A. 10
   B. 20
   C. 30
   D. 40

10. For the second time since beginning to Family Assistance benefits, a recipient fails to comply with the work requirements of her program. Typically, benefits will be suspended for a period of no less than _____.

    A. 30 days
    B. 90 days
    C. 3 months
    D. 6 months

11. A single mother receiving Family Assistance benefits consistently fails to cooperate with the local social services district in establishing the legal father of her child. Typically, the consequence for this failure to cooperate is a

    A. $50 monthly deduction in monthly benefits per each child
    B. 25% reduction in monthly benefits
    C. 50% reduction in monthly benefits
    D. total suspension of benefits

12. A mother and her two children receive Family Assistance. Her grant includes $291 for basic needs, a shelter voucher of $205.00, and a fuel/utility voucher of $54—for a total benefit of $550.00. Recently, the mother received a notice from the Department of Social Services, stating that last year they paid the gas & electric company more than her utility allowance. Under typical conditions, the Department will deduct $_____ from the mother's monthly grant until the overpayment is repaid.

    A. $5.40
    B. $11.00
    C. $55.00
    D. $82.50

13. In general, income disregards for Family Assistance recipients are only applied if wages are reported within _____ of receipt of income.

    A. 48 hours
    B. 5 days
    C. 10 days
    D. 30 days

14. During their first year of residence in New York, U.S. citizens who have relocated to the state

    A. are not eligible for any type of state-funded assistance
    B. receive 50 percent of the New York State benefit or the benefit paid by their prior state of residence, whichever is greater
    C. receive a pro rata benefit that is scaled according to their time of residence
    D. receive the same benefits as any other resident of New York who is a full U.S. citizen

15. The 60-month time limit for Family Assistance would usually apply to a

    A. family with two working parents whose combined income still falls below the poverty test
    B. minor child who lives in a family currently receiving Family Assistance
    C. single-parent family in which the parent is temporarily unable to work due to injury
    D. grandmother who is caring for a child and receiving aid only for the child's needs

16. For applicants of Family Assistance, the add-on rate disregard (47% as of 2002) only applies if the applicant received temporary assistance in one of the _____ months prior to application.

    A. 2   B. 4   C. 6   D. 9

17. A recipient of Family Assistance has failed to comply with his work requirements, and has received notice from the Department of Social Services warning him of this. Generally, the recipient has a period of _____ days in which to provide reasons for this failure, and thereby put and end to the sanctioning process.

    A. 3
    B. 7
    C. 10
    D. 15

18. Which of the following may be denied Temporary Assistance because they refuse to live at home with their parents?
    I. single individuals between 18 and 21 who are not married, are not pregnant, and who have no children, if their parents offer to support them in their home
    II. single individuals between 18 and 21 who unmarried and childless, but pregnant, if their parents offer to support them in their home
    III. single parents between 18 and 21, if their parents offer to support them in their home
    IV. married parents between 18 and 21, if the parents of one offer to support them in their home

    A. I only
    B. I and II
    C. I, II, and III
    D. I, II, III and IV

19. A family has two children enrolled in Learnfare. In the previous academic quarter, each of the children had six unexcused absences from school. Under typical circumstances, the family will be penalized with a

    A. one-time $120 deduction from the monthly benefit
    B. total loss of benefits for one month
    C. $120 deduction from benefits for a period of three months
    D. total loss of benefits for a period of three months

20. Generally, no Temporary Assistance benefits will be given for a minor child who is absent or expected to be absent from a household for more than _____ days without good cause.

    A. 10
    B. 45
    C. 90
    D. 180

21. As of 2002, which of the following resources was NOT exempt from the consideration of an applicant's eligibility for Safety Net Assistance?

    A. A home
    B. $2000 in liquid assets
    C. Standard personal deduction from federal income tax
    D. A car valued up to $4650

22. If a family passes the gross income test for earned income disregards, which of the following would be included in the family's calculated income?
    I. The first $50 spent each month on child support
    II. For six months, the earnings of a child who is a full-time student
    III. For six months, income from a child's participation in a job training program
    IV. A $1000 inheritance from a recently deceased relative

    A. I only
    B. II and III
    C. IV only
    D. I, II, III and IV

23. As of 2002, agencies paying out Safety Net Assistance must have _____ percent of their single-parent caseload meet established work requirements.

    A. 25
    B. 35
    C. 50
    D. 75

24. Under the law, the Department of Social Services in a given area may take up to _____ to issue Expedited Food Stamps to families that qualify.

    A. 24 hours
    B. 48 hours
    C. 7 days
    D. 10 days

25. The state time limit on a client's receipt of cash Safety Net Assistance is _____ months.

    A. 6
    B. 15
    C. 24
    D. 60

KEY (CORRECT ANSWERS)

1.	A	11.	B
2.	C	12.	C
3.	C	13.	C
4.	B	14.	B
5.	A	15.	A
6.	B	16.	B
7.	B	17.	C
8.	D	18.	A
9.	B	19.	C
10.	C	20.	B

21. C
22. C
23. C
24. C
25. C

TEST 2

DIRECTIONS: Each question or incomplete statement is followed by several suggested answers or completions. Select the one the BEST answers the question or completes the statement. *PRINT THE LETTER OF THE CORRECT ANSWER IN THE SPACE AT THE RIGHT.*

1. Compared to the previous state welfare system, programs under the Welfare Reform Act of 1997 generally
    I. provide more limited special needs and emergency grants
    II. place more recipients into workfare, and for more hours
    III. use more non-cash aid in lieu of cash aid
    IV. provide more generous income disregards

    A. I and II
    B. II and IV
    C. II, III and IV
    D. I, II, III and IV

2. In general, temporary assistance will not be given to an unmarried person under 18 who is not attending school, or who does not have a diploma/GED, unless the person is supporting a child

    A. younger than 12 weeks old
    B. younger than 1 year
    C. younger than 3 years
    D. under 18

3. Which of the following would be eligible for Family Assistance benefits?

    A. A family of three which includes a father who suffers from alcoholism
    B. A family of four in which a 19-year-old student is receiving income from a work-study program
    C. A family of five who has already received 60 months of Family Assistance coverage
    D. Immigrant families who arrived in the United States after August 22, 1996.

4. The earned income disregards for Family Assistance recipients would apply to
    I. Social Security income
    II. Veterans' benefits
    III. gifts from relatives
    IV. revenues from the sale of an automobile

    A. I and II
    B. II only
    C. III and IV
    D. I, II, III and IV

5. Temporary Assistance benefits are usually NOT given for a minor child who is absent—or expected to be absent—from a household for a prescribed period of time without good cause. "Good cause" would include
    I. placement in foster care (as long as return to the home is the goal)
    II. attendance at a distant school
    III. extended hospitalization, if return is expected
    IV. living with a close relative

    A. I only   B. I, II, and III
    C. II and IV   D. I, II, III and IV

7

6. A single person is generally NOT eligible for Temporary Assistance if his or her work experience consists of

   A. child care for another person who provides community service
   B. work in the non-profit sector, if no public or private for-profit work is available
   C. subsidized public-sector employment
   D. unsubsidized employment

7. Once an applicant for Temporary Assistance receives a notice of a disability determination, he or she typically has _____ days from the receipt of this notice to request a hearing on the matter.

   A. 5
   B. 10
   C. 30
   D. 90

8. A single person receiving Safety Net assistance qualifies for an earned income disregard. If the person earns $400 a month, and the poverty level for her region and status is $600, the amount of her disregard is $ _____. Assume an add-on rate of 45%.

   A. 90.00
   B. 180.00
   C. 245.00
   D. 270.00

9. Safety Net Assistance recipients who reach the time limit for cash benefits, or who fall into other eligibility categories, receive primarily noncash assistance, including direct vendor payments or two-party checks for rent and utilities. Of the remaining SNA grants to these recipients, about _____ percent will be accessible only through an electronic transfer system.

   A. 20
   B. 40
   C. 60
   D. 80

10. A child enrolled in the Learnfare program must attend school with no more than four unexcused absences during an academic quarter. Usually, an absence will be unexcused if it is due to
    I. a court appearance
    II. a suspension
    III. the child's having to care for a younger sibling
    IV. a family vacation

    A. I and II
    B. II and III
    C. III and IV
    D. I, II, III and IV

11. A household of three has monthly gross earnings of $1080. The standard of need for the household is $664 per month. The household passes both the gross income test and the poverty level test, because the poverty level for the area and status is $1081.66. With an add-on rate of 45%, the family would qualify for a monthly grant of $ _____ after earned income disregards.

    A. 90
    B. 119.50
    C. 222.33
    D. 544.50

12. A Safety Net Assistance recipient, a single man without dependents, has been sanctioned for not complying with the substance abuse treatment requirements of his benefit agreement. After official sanction, the consequence for this recipient is a

    A. $50 monthly deduction from his basic needs benefit
    B. 25% deduction from his overall benefit, including vouchers
    C. total disqualification from benefits
    D. total disqualification from benefits and criminal prosecution, if the substance being abused is illegal

13. The work requirements of state Temporary Assistance programs would be MOST likely to apply to a

    A. person whose presence is required in the home because of the incapacity of another member of the household
    B. person aged 60 or older
    C. 22-year-old who has enrolled as a full-time student at a technical college
    D. single parent caring for a child under a year old, for a 3-month period

14. A Safety Net Assistance recipient may possibly be included in the work participation rates of an agency's program if he or she participates in
    I. community service
    II. unsubsidized employment
    III. attendance in a GED program
    IV. workfare

    A. I and II
    B. II only
    C. II, III and IV
    D. I, II, III and IV

15. A single recipient in Safety Net Assistance has had rent and utilities paid out of his allowance, and received small cash payments equaling about $1 a day for the month. There is still about $29 left in the recipient's allowance. Under the law, this remainder will be paid

    A. to the recipient in cash, but deducted from the next allowance
    B. to the recipient in cash
    C. through an electronic card that can be used to purchase goods and services
    D. back to the social services agency

16. Typically, a person receiving restricted cash Safety Net Assistance will receive a small percentage of the grant in cash. This portion of the benefit is the _____ allowance

    A. personal needs
    B. investment
    C. shelter
    D. utilities

17. Generally, all household members who are applying for Food Stamp benefits must register for employment at the time of application, EXCEPT for members who are working a minimum of _____ hours per week.

    A. 10
    B. 15
    C. 21
    D. 30

18. Mr. Douglas, a Family Assistance recipient, beings working at a job that earns him a gross monthly salary of $400 a month, well below the poverty level. Under the 2002 add-on rate of 47%, his "countable" monthly income would be $ _____.

    A. 90.00
    B. 164.00
    C. 188.00
    D. 212.00

19. Of the following, those eligible for cash Safety Net Assistance include a
    I. single-parent families in which the parent is abusing marijuana
    II. 17-year-old girl without children who has no adult relative to live with
    III. household that has received Family Assistance for a total of 60 months
    IV. family in which the head of the household fails to comply with drug and alcohol screening requirements

    A. I and IV
    B. II only
    C. II and III
    D. I, II, III and IV

20. Generally, a family may qualify for Expedited Food Stamps if they have no liquid resources and their gross monthly income is less than $ _____.

    A. 150.00
    B. 250.00
    C. 300 or 50% less than the poverty level, whichever is highest
    D. 500.00

21. A recipient of Safety Net Assistance fails to attend several consecutive meetings at an outpatient drug rehabilitation center. Because this is the first time he has failed to comply with the drug treatment requirements of the program,

    A. he will be warned by the agency that further failures will result in a suspension of benefits
    B. his benefits will be suspended for no less than 45 days
    C. his benefits will be suspended for no less than 180 days
    D. he will be removed from the caseload

21._____

22. Federal Food Stamp benefits

    A. involve an eligibility level that is generally higher than state Temporary Assistance levels
    B. involve an eligibility level that is generally lower than state Temporary Assistance levels
    C. are automatically terminated once an individual leaves Temporary Assistance
    D. are terminated only if the person's 60-month time limit for Temporary Assistance have expired

22._____

23. For a single parent with a 10-year-old dependent child, the number of minimum weekly work hours required for compliance with Temporary Assistance would generally be

    A. 10
    B. 20
    C. 30
    D. 40

23._____

24. Generally, the review of a client's eligibility for Temporary Assistance takes place every _____ months.

    A. 3
    B. 6
    C. 18
    D. 30

24._____

25. Generally, a single mother's Temporary Assistance benefits are NOT suspended or discontinued if he or she

    A. fails to accept a job offer
    B. refuses to sign a lien on real property that he/she owns
    C. fails to apply for SSI, Unemployment insurance or other available benefits
    D. aids the Child Support Enforcement Unit in establishing paternity for a child born out of wedlock

25._____

KEY (CORRECT ANSWERS)

1. C
2. A
3. B
4. C
5. B

6. A
7. B
8. A
9. D
10. C

11. B
12. C
13. C
14. D
15. C

16. A
17. D
18. B
19. B
20. A

21. B
22. A
23. C
24. B
25. D

EXAMINATION SECTION
TEST 1

DIRECTIONS: Each question or incomplete statement is followed by several suggested answers or completions. Select the one that BEST answers the question or completes the statement. *PRINT THE LETTER OF THE CORRECT ANSWER IN THE SPACE AT THE RIGHT.*

1. Assume that an applicant, obviously under a great deal of stress, talks continuously and rambles, making it difficult for you to determine the exact problem and her need. In order to make the interview more successful, it would be BEST for you to
    A. interrupt the applicant and ask her specific questions in order to get the information you need
    B. tell the applicant that her rambling may be a basic cause of her problem
    C. let the applicant continue talking as long as she wishes
    D. ask the applicant to get to the point because other people are waiting for you

2. A worker must be able to interview clients all day and still be able to listen and maintain interest.
   Of the following, it is MOST important for you to show interest in the client because, if you appear interested,
    A. the client is more likely to appreciate your professional status
    B. the client is more likely to disclose a greater amount of information
    C. the client is less likely to tell lies
    D. you are more likely to gain your supervisor's approval

3. The application process is overwhelming to applicant Ms. M. She is very anxious and is fearful that she does not have all that she needs to be eligible for assistance. As a result, every time she is asked to produce a verifying document during the interview, she fumbles and drops all the other documents to the floor.
   Of the following, the MOST effective method for you to use to complete the application process is to
    A. ask Ms. M not to be so nervous because you cannot get the work done if she fusses so much
    B. take the documents away from Ms. M and do it your self
    C. suggest that Ms. M get a friend to come and help her with the papers
    D. try to calm Ms. M and tell her that you are willing to help her with the papers to get the information you require

4. An applicant for public assistance claims that her husband deserted the family and that she needs money immediately for food since her children have not eaten for two days. Under normal procedure, she has to wait several days before she can be given any money for this purpose. In accordance with departmental policy, no exception can be made in this case.
Of the following, the BEST action for you to take is to
   A. tell her that, according to departmental policy, she cannot be given money immediately
   B. purchase some food for her, using your own funds, so that she can feed her children
   C. take up a collection among co-workers
   D. send her to another center

5. Applicants for public assistance often complain about the length of the application form. They also claim that the questions are too personal, since all they want is money. It is true that the form is long, but the answers to all the questions on the form are needed so that the department can make a decision on eligibility.
When applicants complain, which of the following would be the MOST appropriate action for you to take?
   A. Help such applicants understand that each question has a purpose which will help in the determination of eligibility
   B. Tell such applicants that you agree but that you must comply with regulations because it is your job
   C. Tell such applicants that they should stop complaining if they want you to help
   D. Refer such applicants to a supervisor who will explain agency policy

6. Which one of the following statements BEST describes the primary goal of a worker?
   A. Process as many clients in as short a time as possible
   B. Help his clients
   C. Grow into a more understanding person
   D. Assert his authority

7. Restating a question before the person being interviewed gives an answer to the original question is usually NOT good practice *principally* because
   A. the client will think that you don't know your job
   B. it may confuse the client
   C. the interviewer should know exactly what to ask and how to put the question
   D. it reveals the interviewer's insecurity

8. A white worker can BEST improve his ability to work with black clients if he
   A. tries to forget that the clients are black
   B. tells the black clients that he has no prejudices
   C. becomes aware of the problems black clients face
   D. socializes with black workers in the agency

9. A client warns that if he does not get what he wants he will report you to your supervisor and, if necessary, to the mayor's office.
   Of the following, the MOST appropriate response for you to make in this situation is to
   A. encourage the client to do as he threatens because you know that you are right
   B. call your supervisor in so that the client may confront him
   C. explain to the client how the decision will be made on his request and suggest what action he can take if there is an adverse decision
   D. try to understand the client's problem but tell him that he must not explode in the office because you will have to ask him to leave if he does

Questions 10-20.

DIRECTIONS: Refer to the following Semi-Monthly Family Allowance Schedule and Conversion Table when answering Questions 10 through 20.

SEMI-MONTHLY FAMILY ALLOWANCE SCHEDULE
(Based on Number of Persons in Household)

NUMBER OF PERSONS IN HOUSEHOLD						
One	Two	Three	Four	Five	Six	Each Additional Person
$470.00	$750.00	$1000.00	$1290.00	$1590.00	$1840.00	$25.00

CONVERSION TABLE - WEEKLY TO SEMI-MONTHLY AMOUNTS

DOLLARS				CENTS			
Weekly Amount	Semi-Monthly Amount	Weekly Amount	Semi-Monthly Amount	Weekly Amount	Semi-Monthly Amount	Weekly Amount	Semi-Monthly Amount
$10.00	$21.70	$510.00	$1105.00	$0.10	$0.20	$5.10	$11.10
20.00	43.30	520.00	1126.70	0.20	0.40	5.20	11.30
30.00	65.00	530.00	1148.30	0.30	0.70	5.30	11.50
40.00	86.70	540.00	1170.00	0.40	0.90	5.40	11.70
50.00	108.30	550.00	1191.70	0.50	1.10	5.50	11.90
60.00	130.00	560.00	1213.30	0.60	1.30	5.60	12.10
70.00	151.70	570.00	1235.00	0.70	1.50	5.70	12.40
80.00	173.30	580.00	1256.70	0.80	1.70	5.80	12.60
90.00	195.00	590.00	1278.30	0.90	2.00	5.90	12.80
100.00	216.70	600.00	1300.00	1.00	2.20	6.00	13.00
110.00	238.30	610.00	1321.70	1.10	2.40	6.10	13.20
120.00	260.00	620.00	1343.30	1.20	2.60	6.20	13.40
130.00	281.70	630.00	1365.00	1.30	2.80	6.30	13.70
140.00	303.30	640.00	1386.70	1.40	3.00	6.40	13.90
150.00	325.00	650.00	1408.30	1.50	3.30	6.50	14.10
160.00	346.70	660.00	1430.00	1.60	3.50	6.60	14.30
170.00	368.30	670.00	1451.70	1.70	3.70	6.70	14.50
180.00	390.00	680.00	1473.30	1.80	3.90	6.80	14.70
190.00	411.70	690.00	1495.00	1.90	4.10	6.90	15.00
200.00	433.30	700.00	1516.70	2.00	4.30	7.00	15.20
210.00	455.00	710.00	1538.30	2.10	4.60	7.10	15.40
220.00	476.70	720.00	1560.00	2.20	4.80	7.20	15.60
230.00	498.30	730.00	1581.70	2.30	5.00	7.30	15.80
240.00	520.00	740.00	1603.30	2.40	5.20	7.40	16.00
250.00	541.70	750.00	1625.00	2.50	5.40	7.50	16.30
260.00	563.30	760.00	1646.70	2.60	5.60	7.60	16.50
270.00	585.00	770.00	1668.30	2.70	5.90	7.70	16.70
280.00	606.70	780.00	1690.00	2.80	6.10	7.80	16.90
290.00	628.30	790.00	1711.70	2.90	6.30	7.90	17.10
300.00	650.00	800.00	1733.30	3.00	6.50	8.00	17.30
310.00	671.70	810.00	1755.00	3.10	6.70	8.10	17.60
320.00	693.30	820.00	1776.70	3.20	6.90	8.20	17.80
330.00	715.00	830.00	1798.30	3.30	7.20	8.30	18.00
340.00	736.70	840.00	1820.00	3.40	7.40	8.40	18.20
350.00	783.00	850.00	1841.70	3.50	7.60	8.50	18.40
360.00	780.00	860.00	1863.30	3.60	7.80	8.60	18.60
370.00	801.70	870.00	1885.00	3.70	8.00	8.70	18.90
380.00	823.30	880.00	1906.70	3.80	8.20	8.80	19.10
390.00	845.00	890.00	1928.30	3.90	8.50	8.90	18.30
400.00	866.70	900.00	1950.00	4.00	8.70	9.00	19.50
410.00	888.30	910.00	1971.70	4.10	8.90	9.10	19.70
420.00	910.00	920.00	1993.30	4.20	9.10	9.20	19.90
430.00	931.70	930.00	2015.00	4.30	9.30	9.30	20.20
440.00	953.30	940.00	2036.70	4.40	9.50	9.40	20.40
450.00	975.00	950.00	2058.30	4.50	9.80	9.50	20.60
460.00	996.70	960.00	2080.00	4.60	10.00	9.60	20.80
470.00	1018.30	970.00	2101.70	4.70	10.20	9.70	21.00
480.00	1040.00	980.00	2123.30	4.80	10.40	9.80	21.20
490.00	1061.70	990.00	2145.00	4.90	10.60	9.90	21.50
500.00	1083.30	1000.00	2166.70	5.00	10.80		

NOTE: Questions 10 through 20 are to be answered SOLELY on the basis of the Schedule and Table given above and the information and case situations given below.

Questions 10 through 14 are based on Case Situation #1.
Questions 15 through 20 are based on Case Situation #2.

Public assistance grants are computed on a semi-monthly basis. This means that all figures are first broken down into semi-monthly amounts, and that when a client receives a check twice a month, each semi-monthly check covers his requirements for a period of approximately 2-1/6 weeks. The grants are computed by means of the following procedures.

1. Determine the semi-monthly allowance for the family from the Semi-Monthly Family Allowance Schedule.
2. Determine total semi-monthly income by deducting from the semi-monthly gross earnings (the wages or salary *before* payroll deductions) all semi-monthly expenses for federal, state, and city income taxes, Social Security payments, State Disability Insurance payments, union dues, cost of transportation, and $10.00 per work day for lunch.
3. Add the semi-monthly allowance and the semi-monthly rent (monthly rent must be divided in half).
4. Subtract the semi-monthly income (if there is any income).
5. The formula for computing the semi-monthly grant is:
   Family Allowance + Rent (semi-monthly)
   – Total Income (semi-monthly)
   = Amount of Grant (semi-monthly)
6. Refer to the Conversion Table in order to convert weekly amounts into semi-monthly amounts.

CASE SITUATION #1

The Smiths receive public assistance. The family includes John Smith, his wife Barbara, and their four children. They occupy a five-room apartment for which the rent is $1050.00 per month. Mr. Smith is employed as a cleaner and his gross wages are $1000 per week. He is employed 5 days a week and spends $7.00 a day carfare. He buys his lunches. The following weekly deductions are made from his salary:

Social Security	$60.00
Disability Benefits	3.80
Federal Income Tax	43.00
State Income Tax	28.00
City Income Tax	10.00

CASE SITUATION #2

The Jones family receives public assistance. The family includes Steven and Diane Jones and their two children. They occupy a four-room apartment for which the rental is $850.00 a month. Mr. Jones is employed as a handyman, and his gross wages are $900 per week. He is employed 4 days a week and spends $7.00 a day carfare. He buys his lunches. He has the following weekly deductions made from his salary:

    Social Security $40.00
    Disability Benefits   2.70
    Federal Income Tax   38.90
    State Income Tax   20.50
    City Income Tax   6.20

10. The weekly amount that Mr. Smith contributes towards Social Security, Disability Benefits, and income taxes is
    A. $313.70   B. $231.40   C. $144.80   D. $106.80

11. The semi-monthly family allowance for the Smith family is
    A. $1290.00   B. $1590.00   C. $1840.00   D. $1845.00

12. What is the total of semi-monthly expenses related to Mr. Smith's employment which will be deducted from semi-monthly gross earnings to compute semi-monthly income?
    A. $497.80   B. $422.00   C. $389.50   D. $229.80

13. Which of the following amounts is the total semi-monthly income for the Smith family?
    A. $2166.70   B. $2000.00   C. $1668.90   D. $1004.40

14. The amount of the grant which the Smith family is entitled to receive is
    A. $2365.00   B. $1840.00   C. $1392.20   D. $696.10

15. The weekly amount that Mr. Jones contributes towards Social Security, Disability Benefits, and income taxes is
    A. $108.30   B. $176.30   C. $234.30   D. $234.70

16. The semi-monthly family allowance for the Jones family is
    A. $750.00   B. $1000.00   C. $1220.00   D. $1290.00

17. The total of semi-monthly expenses related to Mr. Jones' employment which will be deducted from semi-monthly gross earnings is
    A. $172.30   B. $189.30   C. $382.00   D. $407.20

18. Which of the following amounts is the total semi-monthly income for the Jones family? 18._____
      A. $1282.00   B. $1553.20   C. $1568.00   D. $2122.30

19. The grant which the Jones family will receive is 19._____
      A. $147.00   B. $294.00   C. $1290.00   D. $1715.00

20. If Mrs. Jones' monthly rent had been $1050, what would the amount of the grant be? 20._____
      A. $247.00   B. $494.00   C. $772.00   D. $1822.00

KEY (CORRECT ANSWERS)

1. A   11. C
2. B   12. A
3. D   13. C
4. A   14. D
5. A   15. A

6. B   16. D
7. B   17. C
8. C   18. C
9. C   19. A
10. C   20. A

TEST 2

DIRECTIONS: Each question or incomplete statement is followed by several suggested answers or completions. Select the one that BEST answers the question or completes the statement. *PRINT THE LETTER OF THE CORRECT ANSWER IN THE SPACE AT THE RIGHT.*

Questions 1-5.

DIRECTIONS: Each of Questions 1 through 5 consists of information given in outline form and four sentences labeled A, B, C, and D. For each question, choose the one sentence which CORRECTLY expresses the information given in outline form and which also displays PROPER English usage.

1. Client's Name - Joanna Jones
    Number of Children - 3
    Client's Income - None
    Client's Marital Status - Single
    A. Joanna Jones is an unmarried client with three children who have no income.
    B. Joanna Jones, who is single and has no income, a client she has three children.
    C. Joanna Jones, whose three children are clients, is single and has no income.
    D. Joanna Jones, who has three children, is an unmarried client with no income.

1.___

2. Client's Name - Bertha Smith
    Number of Children - 2
    Client's Rent - $1050 per month
    Number of Rooms- 4
    A. Bertha Smith, a client, pays $1050 per month for her four rooms with two children.
    B. Client Bertha Smith has two children and pays $1050 per month for four rooms.
    C. Client Bertha Smith is paying $1050 per month for two children with four rooms.
    D. For four rooms and two children, Client Bertha Smith pays $1050 per month.

2.___

3. Name of Employee - Cynthia Dawes
    Number of Cases Assigned - 9
    Date Cases Were Assigned - 12/16
    Number of Assigned Cases Completed - 8
    A. On December 16, employee Cynthia Dawes was assigned nine cases; she has completed eight of these cases.
    B. Cynthia Dawes, employee on December 16, assigned nine cases, completed eight.
    C. Being employed on December 16, Cynthia Dawes completed eight of nine assigned cases.
    D. Employee Cynthia Dawes, she was assigned nine cases and completed eight, on December 16.

3.___

4. Place of Audit - Broadway Center
    Names of Auditors - Paul Cahn, Raymond Perez
    Date of Audit - 11/20
    Number of Cases Audited - 41
    A. On November 20, at the Broadway Center 41 cases was audited by auditors Paul Cahn and Raymond Perez.
    B. Auditors Raymond Perez and Paul Cahn has audited 41 cases at the Broadway

4.___

Center, on November 20.
   C. At the Broadway Center, on November 20, auditors Paul Cahn and Raymond Perez audited 41 cases.
   D. Auditors Paul Cahn and Raymond Perez at the Broadway Center, on November 20, is auditing 41 cases.

5. Name of Client - Barbra Levine   5._____
   Client's Monthly Income - $2100
   Client's Monthly Expenses - $4520
   A. Barbra Levine is a client, her monthly income is $2100 and her monthly expenses is $4520.
   B. Barbra Levine's monthly income is $2100 and she is a client, with whose monthly expenses are $4520.
   C. Barbra Levine is a client whose monthly income is $2100 and whose monthly expenses are $4520.
   D. Barbra Levine, a client, is with a monthly income which is $2100 and monthly expenses which are $4520.

Questions 6-10.

DIRECTIONS: Questions 6 through 10 are to be answered SOLELY on the basis of the information contained in the following passage.

Any person who is living in New York City and is otherwise eligible may be granted public assistance whether or not he has New York State residence. However, since New York City does not contribute to the cost of assistance granted to persons who are without State residence, the cases of all recipients must be formally identified as to whether or not each member of the household has State residence.

To acquire State residence a person must have resided in New York State continuously for one year. Such residence is not lost unless the person is out of the State continuously for a period of one year or longer. Continuous residence does not include any period during which the individual is a patient in a hospital, an inmate of a public institution or of an incorporated private institution, a resident on a military reservation or a minor residing in a boarding home while under the care of an authorized agency. Receipt of public assistance does not prevent a person from acquiring State residence. State residence, once acquired, is not lost because of absence from the State while a person is serving in the U.S. Armed Forces or the Merchant Marine; nor does a member of the family of such a person lose State residence while living with or near that person in these circumstances.

Each person, regardless of age, acquires or loses State residence as an individual. There is no derivative State residence except for an infant at the time of birth. He is deemed to have State residence if he is in the custody of both parents and either one of them has State residence, or if the parent having custody of him has State residence.

6. According to the above passage, an infant is deemed to have New York State residence at the time of his birth *if*
   A. he is born in New York State but neither of his parents is a resident
   B. he is in the custody of only one parent, who is not a resident, but his other parent is a resident
   C. his brother and sister are residents
   D. he is in the custody of both his parents but only one of them is a resident

7. The Jones family consists of five members. Jack and Mary Jones have lived in New York State continuously for the past eighteen months after having lived in Ohio since they were born. Of their three children, one was born ten months ago and has been in the custody of his parents since birth. Their second child lived in Ohio until six months ago and then moved in with his parents. Their third child had never lived in New York until he moved with his parents to New York eighteen months ago. However, he entered the armed forces one month later and has not lived in New York since that time.
   Based on the above passage, how many members of the Jones family are New York State residents?
   A. 2 B. 3 C. 4 D. 5

8. Assuming that each of the following individuals has lived continuously in New York State for the past year, and has never previously lived in the State, which one of them is a New York State resident?
   A. Jack Salinas, who has been an inmate in a State correctional facility for six months of the year
   B. Fran Johnson, who has lived on an Army base for the entire year
   C. Arlene Snyder, who married a non-resident during the past year
   D. Gary Phillips, who was a patient in a Veterans Administration hospital for the entire year

9. The above passage implies that the reason for determining whether or not a recipient of public assistance is a State resident is that
   A. the cost of assistance for non-residents is not a New York City responsibility
   B. non-residents living in New York City are not eligible for public assistance
   C. recipients of public assistance are barred from acquiring State residence
   D. New York City is responsible for the full cost of assistance to recipients who are residents

10. Assume that the Rollins household in New York City consists of six members at the present time - Anne Rollins, her three children, her aunt and her uncle. Anne Rollins and one of her children moved to New York City seven months ago. Neither of them had previously lived in New York State. Her other two children have lived in New York City continuously for the past two years, as has her aunt. Anne Rollins' uncle had lived in New York City continuously for many years until two years ago. He then entered the armed forces and has returned to New York City within the past month.
    Based on the above passage, how many members of the Rollins' household are New York State residents?
    A. 2 B. 3 C. 4 D. 6

11. You are interviewing a client to determine whether financial assistance should be continued and you find that what he is telling you does not agree exactly with your records.
    Of the following, the BEST way to handle this situation is to
    A. recommend that his public assistance payments be stopped, since you have caught him lying to you
    B. tell the client about the points of disagreement and ask him if he can clear them up
    C. give the client the benefit of the doubt and recommend continuation of his payments
    D. show the client the records and warn him that he must either tell the truth or lose his benefits

11.____

12. An applicant for public assistance gets angry at some of the questions you must ask her.
    Of the following, the BEST way to handle this situation is to
    A. assume that she is trying to hide something, and end the interview
    B. skip the questions that bother her and come back to them at the end of the interview
    C. tell her that she must either answer the question or leave
    D. explain to her that you are required to get answers to all the questions in order to be able to help her

12.____

13. At the end of an interview to determine whether financial assistance should be continued, the client offers to take you to lunch.
    Of the following, the BEST response to such an invitation is to
    A. tell the client that you do not take bribes and report the matter to your supervisor
    B. accept the invitation if you have the time, but do not let it influence your recommendation as to his eligibility for continuing public assistance
    C. politely refuse the invitation, and do not let it influence your recommendation as to his continuing eligibility for public assistance
    D. point out to the client that his budget does not include money for entertainment

13.____

Questions 14-18.

DIRECTIONS: Questions 14 through 18 are to be answered SOLELY on the basis of the information, the assumptions, and the table given below.

Each question describes an applicant family. You are to determine into which of the four categories (A, B, C, or D) each of the applicant families should be placed. In order to do this, you must match the description of the applicant family with the factors determining eligibility for each of the four categories. Each applicant family must meet ALL of the criteria for the category.

ASSUMPTIONS FOR ALL QUESTIONS
   The information in the following tables does NOT necessarily reflect actual practice in the Department of Social Services.
   1. The date of application is January 25.
      Each applicant family that cannot be placed in categories A, B, or C must be placed in category D.
   2. A *dependent child* is a child who is less than 18 years of age, or less than 21 years of age if attending school full time, who depends upon its parents for support.
   3. A mother in a family with one or more dependent children is not expected to work and her work status is not to be considered in establishing the category of the family.

CATEGORY OF APPLICANT FAMILY	FACTORS DETERMINING ELIGIBILITY

A	1. There is at least one dependent child in the home.
	2. Children are deprived of parental support because father is:
	   (a) Deceased
	   (b) Absent from the home
	   (c) Incapacitated due to medically verified illness
	   (d) Over age 65
	   (e) Not fully employed because of verified ill health
	3. Parents or guardians reside in the same home as the children.
	4. Applicant family must have resided in the State for a period of one year or more.

B	1. There is at least one dependent child in the home. 2. Both parents are in the home and are not incapacitated. 3. Both parents are the children's natural parents. 4. Father unemployed or works less than 70 hours per month. 5. Father has recent work history. 6. Father not currently receiving Unemployment Insurance Benefits. 7. Father available and willing to work. 8. Applicant family must have resided in the State for a period of one year or more.
C	1. There is a war veteran in the home. 2. Applicant families do not meet the criteria for Categories A or B.
D	Applicant families do not meet the criteria for Categories A, B, or C

14. Woman, aged 52, with child 6 years old who she states was left in her home at the age of 2. Woman states child is her niece, and that she has no knowledge of whereabouts of parents or any other relatives. Both woman and child have resided in the State since June 15. 14. ___

15. Married couple with 2 dependent children at home. Family has resided in the State for the last 5 years. Wife cannot work. Husband, veteran of Gulf War, can work only 15 hours a week due to kidney ailment (verified). 15. ___

16. Married couple, both aged 35, with 3 dependent children at home, 1 of whom is 17 years of age. Wife available for work and presently working 2 days a week, 7 hours each day. Husband, who was laid off two weeks ago, is not eligible for Unemployment Insurance Benefits. Family has resided in the State since January 1, 2002.

16. ____

17. Married couple with 1 dependent child at home. They have resided in the State since January 25, 2001. Wife must remain home to take care of child. Husband veteran of Gulf War. Husband is available for work on a limited basis because of heart condition which has been verified. A second child, a married 17-year-old son, lives in California.

17. ____

18. Married couple with 2 children, ages 6 and 12, at home. Family has resided in the State since June 2, 1998. Wife not available for work. Husband, who served in the Iraqi War, was laid off 3 weeks ago and is receiving Unemployment Insurance Benefits of $500.00 weekly.

18. ____

19. Of the following, the MOST important reason for referring a public assistance client for employment or training is to
    A. give him self-confidence
    B. make him self-supporting
    C. have him learn a new trade
    D. take him off the streets

19. ____

20. Sometimes clients become silent during interviews.
    Of the following, the MOST probable reason for such silence is that the client is
    A. getting ready to tell a lie
    B. of low intelligence and does not know the answers to your questions
    C. thinking things over or has nothing more to say on the subject
    D. wishing he were not on welfare

20. ____

KEY (CORRECT ANSWERS)

1. D	6. D	11. B	16. B
2. B	7. B	12. D	17. A
3. A	8. C	13. C	18. C
4. C	9. A	14. D	19. B
5. C	10. C	15. A	20. C

EXAMINATION SECTION
TEST 1

DIRECTIONS: Each question or incomplete statement is followed by several suggested answers or completions. Select the one that BEST answers the question or completes the statement. *PRINT THE LETTER OF THE CORRECT ANSWER IN THE SPACE AT THE RIGHT.*

1. Of the following, an important goal of the reorganization of a human services agency is to

    A. strengthen the centralization of services at agency headquarters
    B. provide services within the neighborhoods according to local needs
    C. equalize the distribution of responsibilities between headquarters and neighborhood offices
    D. give more authority and responsibility to neighborhood offices than to headquarters

2. The one of the following which is NOT a purpose of the movement toward decentralization of city government is to

    A. reduce citizen alienation
    B. bolster city services
    C. respond to local needs
    D. discourage the local power structure

3. Of the following, the MOST desirable way to strengthen the capacity of communities to contribute to the solution of their own problems is to

    A. encourage participation of local residents in service planning and delivery
    B. establish city-wide job training programs
    C. reduce technical assistance to local small business so that they will learn by experience
    D. make local residents accountable to government agencies for funds and services provided

4. In organizing the residents of a disadvantaged neighborhood to develop projects for community improvement, the MOST effective of the following approaches is to

    A. concentrate on the group with most members
    B. devote more attention to groups which have vested interests
    C. try to include all groups
    D. give special consideration to official groups

5. The one of the following which has been the MOST common problem which occurs when attempts are made to obtain community participation in a project such as a neighborhood improvement program is

    A. domination by an aggressive but unrepresentative group
    B. public opposition by representatives of government agencies
    C. fragmentation and disruption of community services
    D. serious deterioration in the quality of services

6. Of the following, the MOST important aim of the community organizer in his early contacts with a community group should be to

   A. build a core of common interests
   B. establish himself as a forceful leader who can make decisions
   C. inform the group of its legal rights
   D. curb discussion of opposing viewpoints in order to develop harmonious relations

7. The one of the following which is the BEST method of encouraging neighborhood people to attend a community meeting is to

   A. send out notices at least a week in advance
   B. set up an agenda that deals with issues of serious local concern
   C. invite a prominent public figure to address the meeting
   D. send invitations to community people with similar viewpoints on the problem to be discussed

8. A basic difference between pure experimental research and action research is that experimental research is primarily concerned with the analysis of data for scientific or technological generalization, while action research is

   A. based on the results of trial and error
   B. designed to effect improvement in an on–going process
   C. intuitive rather than scientific in nature
   D. primarily concerned with the analysis of data for universal generalization

9. Assume that a community worker is assigned to organize a client group to participate in planning for services they particularly need.
   Of the following, it would be LEAST important for the organizer to become familiar with the

   A. local store owners
   B. neighborhood resources
   C. potential leaders
   D. informal leaders

10. Of the following, the factor which is MOST important in encouraging a high level of local participation in community projects is the

    A. degree of sophistication of the local people
    B. attitudes of the community development workers towards the local people
    C. amount of money available for training
    D. amount of time available for stimulation of community interest

11. Assume that you are the discussion leader of a meeting of a group of residents of a poverty area, many of whom are against a proposal to locate a methadone maintenance treatment center in the neighborhood.
    The BEST way for you to assist the group is to help them FIRST to

    A. get to know each other on an informal basis
    B. understand the overall background of the drug problem and the need for such a facility in the community
    C. concentrate on all the issues until they iron out conflicting viewpoints
    D. discuss the pros and cons briefly, take a vote, and accept the decision of the majority

12. Of the following, the MOST important aim of the community development process is primarily to strengthen the

    A. long–established social and political pattern of relationships
    B. influence of dominant ethnic and religious groups
    C. long–standing power of traditional central government
    D. positive impulses of people working toward a common goal

13. One method of influencing human behavior is based upon an optimistic belief in human potential for development and betterment.
    Workers in the human services who apply this method expect that it will

    A. awaken initiative in clients
    B. demand a pre–chosen response from clients
    C. give clients a spirit of competition
    D. get clients to accept new ideas

14. The community development process is MOST effective when

    A. final decisions are made solely by the community development expediters
    B. a firm plan is made after a project gets under way
    C. decisions are left in the hands of community people
    D. militant factions are permitted to take a firm stand

15. Of the following, the MOST significant indication that an organizer of a community group has done an effective job would be a situation where the group

    A. continues to grow in size and strength after the organizer has departed
    B. disperses after the organizer has departed because it has fulfilled its purpose
    C. attains its goals only under the organizer's guidance
    D. has a warm and friendly relationship with the organizer

16. The MAIN purpose of group discussion of community issues by local residents is to

    A. present a predetermined point of view
    B. provide an outlet for release of the participants' aggressions
    C. consider and work through common problems
    D. improve relationships among participants

17. Of the following, the MOST important reason why the community development worker in a disadvantaged community of a major metropolis should seek to understand the motivations of the local residents is that he will be more capable of assisting them in developing

    A. self–help activities
    B. projects which will get publicity
    C. an overall master plan
    D. projects which do not require technical assistance

18. At certain times, there is a tendency for community groups to disregard democratic procedures in making decisions, particularly in a situation where

    A. action depends on availability of community services
    B. the executive board makes the decision
    C. there is need for speedy action
    D. there is no sound basis for the decision

18.____

19. The employment of residents of poverty areas with little or no educational qualifications to assist professional staff members in working with clients of human services agencies is GENERALLY considered

    A. *advisable,* mainly because local paraprofessionals can be expected to bridge the gap between the middle class professional worker and lower class recipients of service
    B. *inadvisable,* mainly because the employment of workers who are not professionals will lower the professional standards of the agency's staff
    C. *advisable,* mainly because employment of paraprofes–sional local residents will save agency funds
    D. *inadvisable,* mainly because clients will receive services of poorer quality than services provided by professional workers

19.____

20. The social work activist who was a leader in the movement to achieve welfare reform by organizing welfare clients and encouraging the poor to demand their legal rights to public assistance is (was)

    A. Saul Alinsky
    B. Richard Cloward
    C. Bertram Beck
    D. Jesse Gray

20.____

Questions 21–26.

DIRECTIONS: Questions 21 through 26 are to be answered SOLELY on the basis of the following passage.

Too often in the past, society has accepted the existing social welfare programs, preferring to tinker with refinements when fundamental reform was in order. It has been a *demeaning*, degrading welfare system in which the instrument of government was wrongfully and *ineptly* used. It has been a system which has only alienated those forced to benefit from it and demoralized those who had to administer it at the level where the pain was clearly visible.

There is a need to put this nation on a course in which cash benefits, providing a basic level or support, are conferred in such a way as to intrude as little as possible into privacy and self–respect. It is difficult to define a basic level of support, no matter how high or low it might be set. In the end, however, the decision is not determined so much by how much is truly adequate for a family to meet all of its needs, but by the resources available to carry out the promise. That may be a harsh fact of life but it is also just that—a fact of life.

21. Of the following, the MOST suitable title for the above passage would be

    A. THE NEED FOR GOVERNMENT CONTROL OF WELFARE
    B. DETERMINING THE BASIC LEVEL OF SUPPORT
    C. THE NEED FOR WELFARE REFORM
    D. THE ELIMINATION OF WELFARE PROGRAMS

22. In this passage, the author's GREATEST criticism of the welfare system is that it is too

    A. disrespectful of recipients
    B. expensive to administer
    C. limited by regulations
    D. widespread in application

23. According to the passage, the basic level of support is ACTUALLY determined by

    A. how much is required for a family to meet all of its needs
    B. the age of the recipients
    C. how difficult it is to administer the program
    D. the economic resources of the nation

24. In this passage, the author does NOT argue for

    A. a work Incentive system
    B. a basic level of support
    C. cash benefits
    D. the privacy of recipients

25. As used in the above passage, the italicized word *demeaning* means MOST NEARLY

    A. ineffective
    B. expensive
    C. overburdened
    D. humiliating

26. As used in the above passage, the italicized, word *ineptly* means MOST NEARLY

    A. foolishly
    B. unsuccessfully
    C. unskillfully
    D. unhappily

Questions 27–30.

DIRECTIONS: Questions 27 through 30 are to be answered SOLELY on the basis of the following paragraph.

The unemployment rate, which counts those unemployed in the sense that they are actively looking for work and unable to find it, gives a relatively *superficial* index of economic conditions in a community. A better index is the subemployment rate which includes the unemployment rate and also includes those working part–time while they are trying to get full–time work; those heads of households under 65 years of age who earn less than $240 per week working full–time, and those individuals under 65 who are not heads of households and earn less than $220 per week in a full–time job; and an estimate of the males *not counted,* which is a very real concern in ghetto areas.

27. Of the following, the MOST suitable title for the above paragraph would be

   A. EMPLOYMENT IN THE UNITED STATES
   B. PART-TIME WORKERS AND THE ECONOMY
   C. THE LABOR MARKET AND THE COMMUNITY
   D. TWO INDICATORS OF ECONOMIC CONDITIONS

28. On the basis of the paragraph, which of the following statements is CORRECT? The

   A. unemployment rate includes everyone who is not fully employed
   B. subemployment rate is higher than the unemployment rate
   C. unemployment rate gives a more complex picture of the economic situation than the subemployment rate
   D. subemployment rate indicates how many part-time workers are dissatisfied with the number of hours they work per week

29. As used in the above paragraph, the italicized word *superficial* means MOST NEARLY

   A. exaggerated   B. official
   C. surface   D. current

30. According to the paragraph, which of the following is included in the subemployment rate?

   A. Everyone who is unemployed
   B. All part-time workers
   C. Everyone under 65 who earns less than $224 per week in a full-time job
   D. All heads of households who earn less than $240 per week in a full-time job

KEY (CORRECT ANSWERS)

1. B	11. B	21. C
2. D	12. D	22. A
3. A	13. A	23. D
4. C	14. C	24. A
5. A	15. A	25. D
6. A	16. C	26. C
7. B	17. A	27. D
8. B	18. C	28. B
9. A	19. A	29. C
10. B	20. B	30. C

TEST 2

DIRECTIONS: Each question or incomplete statement is followed by several suggested answers or completions. Select the one that BEST answers the question or completes the statement. *PRINT THE LETTER OF THE CORRECT ANSWER IN THE SPACE AT THE RIGHT.*

1. The one of the following which accounts for the LARGEST portion of the budget of the Human Resources Administration is 1.____

   A. personnel and support services
   B. public assistance and medicaid
   C. services to children and youth
   D. community organization and development

2. According to the latest statistics published by the U. S. Department of Health, Education and Welfare, the state which spent the LARGEST amount of money per person for public assistance is 2.____

   A. California   B. Massachusetts
   C. Pennsylvania   D. New York

3. According to the MOST recent U.S. Census Bureau Report, the group living in New York City which has the lowest income level is the 3.____

   A. Blacks   B. Puerto Ricans
   C. Dominicans   D. Haitians

4. The group that contains the LARGEST number of individuals receiving public assistance is 4.____

   A. children under working age
   B. unemployed heads of families
   C. the aged, disabled, and blind
   D. unemployed single persons

5. A MAJOR difficulty faced by new arrivals to cities since 1970 which did not exist for earlier European immigrants is the fact that the majority of present–day arrivals 5.____

   A. must forfeit their native culture patterns
   B. have an obviously darker skin color than most longtime residents
   C. have little education
   D. have few occupational skills

6. Generally speaking, low–income persons do not make maximum use of opportunities and services available to them MAINLY because 6.____

   A. most paraprofessional workers, while sincere in the desire to serve, are unable to reach the hard core
   B. much of the routine paperwork in public assistance programs is now assigned to paraprofessional workers
   C. they have become increasingly self–reliant and prefer to cope with their problems without help
   D. they lack the confidence and know–how necessary to make their needs known to the proper persons or agencies

7. The one of the following problems which has once again become a serious concern of youth services agencies is the   7.____

   A. increasing high school drop-out rate
   B. resurgence of fighting youth gangs
   C. spread of youth narcotics addiction
   D. lack of recreation programs

8. Of the following, the MOST recent development with regard to welfare recipients is   8.____

   A. introduction of the declaration of need instead of an investigation of eligibility
   B. a major emphasis on employment programs
   C. increased use of casework therapy and psychiatric counseling
   D. acceptance of narcotics addicts for home relief

9. According to a recent decision by a federal court, regular reporting at state employment service offices to pick up checks or accept work can NO LONGER be required of recipients of   9.____

   A. Aid to the Disabled
   B. Home Relief
   C. Aid to Dependent Children
   D. Medicaid

10. A BASIC objective of the proposal for revenue sharing under consideration by the U.S. Congress is to provide   10.____

    A. state and local governments with new sources of revenue from the federal government and greater control over how this revenue is spent
    B. the federal government with greater control over spending of certain federally-raised tax revenues
    C. safeguards against improper allocation of funds by state and local officials and incentives to states for reporting violations by local government
    D. a method of sharing federal revenue with the states and localities in accordance with their required expenditures for public assistance and social welfare services

11. The component of the human services agency which sets policy for the administration, coordination, and allocation of funds for community action programs is the   11.____

    A. Community Development Agency
    B. Department of Social Services
    C. Council on Poverty
    D. Manpower and Career Development Agency

12. The policies of the Council Against Poverty are carried out by the   12.____

    A. Community Development Agency
    B. Manpower and Career Development Agency
    C. Department of Social Services
    D. Neighborhood Manpower Service Centers

13. The reorganization of the human services agency has established the unit of organization for provisions of services at the neighborhood level as the 13._____

   A. designated poverty area
   B. human resources district
   C. catchment area
   D. census tract

14. The Child Development Commission established by the Agency for Child Development can BEST be described as a group comprised of 14._____

   A. professionals in child psychology and early childhood education who will consult with Agency staff members on policy and programs
   B. parents, community organizations, and concerned citizens who will help the Agency determine, review, and modify policies and guidelines for childcare services
   C. child–care experts who will provide technical assistance to private groups that want to develop early childhood centers
   D. professionals who will offer health and nutrition consultation and a variety of support and referral services for children and parents

15. The BASIC purpose of the office of Community Social Services in the Department of Social Services is to 15._____

   A. help local community leaders establish liaison with private social service agencies in their communities
   B. determine the social service needs of each community and provide services in accordance with these needs
   C. provide information and referral to all HRA services existing in a particular community and to services provided by other city agencies and private organizations
   D. assume responsibility for a variety of social services mandated by federal and state regulations

16. The Social Service Exchange is CORRECTLY described as a 16._____

   A. recruitment center for the training and placement of volunteers for social and health agencies
   B. center which maintains a central index of case records of families and individuals known to social and health agencies
   C. center which provides information about and makes referrals to social and health agencies and proprietary nursing homes
   D. confidential advisory service to help potential contributors evaluate local voluntary health and welfare agencies

17. Which one of the following is an IMPORTANT purpose of the formation of the Office of Special Services for Children in the Department of Social Services? 17._____

   A. Greater programmatic integration of the protective and supportive services to children who are abused, neglected, dependent, delinquent, or in need of services
   B. More professional attention to child abuse cases and prompt court action to penalize parents of abused or neglected children
   C. Separation of programs and facilities for children adjudged to be delinquent from special services for other dependent, abused, or neglected children
   D. Increased attention to home–finding and foster care and adoption services rather than institutional care for dependent children

18. The one of the following which is provided by the Department of Social Services for current, former, and potential public assistance recipients ONLY is _____ services.

    A. information
    B. child welfare
    C. referral
    D. homemaker

19. A MAJOR goal of the Department of Social Services which is part of the reorganization and the separation of income maintenance from social services is to

    A. limit the provision of public social services to those persons who are eligible for public assistance
    B. make public social services available to all persons, whether or not they require financial assistance
    C. refer clients who require social services to private agencies wherever possible
    D. emphasize casework treatment and referral of clients for psychiatric services rather than programs to effect environmental change

20. Of the following, the MAIN functions of the Manpower and Career Development Agency (MCDA) of a human services agency are to

    A. train the unskilled, upgrade existing skills, develop job opportunities, and place newly-trained people in jobs
    B. operate manpower, recruitment, and testing centers under contract with private organizations
    C. provide remedial education and follow-up for dis-advantaged potential college students and vocational testing and counseling for veterans and ex-addicts
    D. provide job development, interviewing and placement, and manpower research services

Questions 21–25.

DIRECTIONS: Questions 21 through 25 are to be answered SOLELY on the diagram presented below.

HOW THE INNER–CITY FAMILY IN URBANVILLE SPENDS ITS MONEY

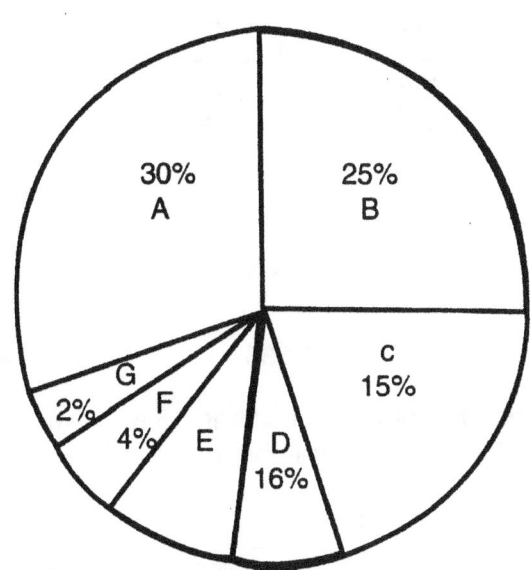

A. Food
B. Shelter
C. Clothing
D. Household Operation
E. Medical Care
F. Transportation
G. Miscellaneous

21. According to the above diagram, the percentage spent on medical care is   21._____

   A. 7%   B. 8%   C. 16%   D. 18%

22. According to the above diagram, the total percentage spent on food, shelter, and clothing is   22._____

   A. 55%   B. 60%   C. 70%   D. 75%

23. In a typical period, if the family spent $60 on transportation, how much did it spend on household operation?   23._____

   A. $240   B. $384   C. $600   D. $960

24. If the family income is $250 a week, how much does it spend on transportation each year?   24._____

   A. $120   B. $520   C. $1,200   D. $5,200

25. Assume that the annual income of a family was $10,800 for several years. Last year, the income went up 5%, and the family then tripled the typical percentage for household operation.   25._____
    The amount spent on this item last year was MOST NEARLY

   A. $1,782   B. $2,268   C. $2,592   D. $5,442

Questions 26–30.

DIRECTIONS: Questions 26 through 30 are to be answered SOLELY on the basis of the table presented below.

AFDC FAMILY MEMBERS IN URBANVILLE
Referred to and Enrolled in WIN Program, 2001-2002

Family Member	Referred		Enrolled	
	2001	2002	2001	2002
Mother	1,091	1,306	730	877
Father	743	950	520	731
Child, age 16 and over	170	222	150	184

26. According to the above table, how many AFDC family members were referred to WIN in 2002?

    A. 1,792　　B. 2,004　　C. 2,388　　D. 2,478

27. According to the above table, the number of AFDC children 16 and over who were enrolled in WIN in 2002 was GREATER than the number enrolled in 2001 by

    A. 12　　B. 34　　C. 38　　D. 52

28. According to the above table, the number of AFDC mothers who were enrolled in 2002 INCREASED over the number enrolled in 2001 MOST NEARLY by

    A. 20%　　B. 32%　　C. 54%　　D. 83%

29. In 2003, if the number of AFDC mothers referred to WIN increases 5% over 2002, the number of fathers referred increases 8% over 2002, and the number of children referred increases 5% over 2002, the TOTAL number of AFDC family members that will be referred in 2003 is MOST NEARLY

    A. 1,424　　B. 1,524　　C. 3,130　　D. 3,990

30. According to the above table, the percentage of AFDC fathers NOT enrolled in WIN in 2002 of the number referred that year is MOST NEARLY

    A. 23%　　B. 25%　　C. 71%　　D. 77%

KEY (CORRECT ANSWERS)

1. B	11. C	21. B
2. D	12. A	22. C
3. D	13. B	23. A
4. A	14. B	24. B
5. B	15. B	25. D
6. D	16. B	26. D
7. B	17. A	27. B
8. B	18. D	28. A
9. C	19. B	29. C
10. A	20. A	30. A

EXAMINATION SECTION
TEST 1

DIRECTIONS: Each question or incomplete statement is followed by several suggested answers or completions. Select the one that BEST answers the question or completes the statement. *PRINT THE LETTER OF THE CORRECT ANSWER IN THE SPACE AT THE RIGHT.*

1. One day an elderly man asks you if he can apply for Social Security at the welfare office.
   Your response should be to
   A. tell him that it is foolish to think he can apply for Social Security at the welfare office
   B. take him back to his apartment because he is too old to be roaming the streets asking questions
   C. explain that Social Security is a federal program and direct him to the nearest Social Security office
   D. call his daughter and tell her that the family should take better care of their father

   1.____

2. One of your duties is to occasionally visit clients. On one occasion, you visit Mrs. B., who needs assistance in referral of her children for day care so that she may enter a job training program. She has postponed completing the referral.
   What should you do in this situation?
   A. Tell her that if she doesn't hurry there will be no room at the day care center and the training program will be closed
   B. Make the arrangements and tell Mrs. B. that she should do what you say
   C. Remember that all people who ask for help are not always ready to receive it and continue to allow Mrs. B. to complete the referral by herself
   D. The next time Mrs. B. asks for help, see that she gets it as slowly as possible

   2.____

3. Assume that you are trying to contact a community group to offer to meet with their representative to explain a new agency policy about intake procedures.
   In order to "get your message across," you should
   A. write a short concise letter explaining why you want to meet with them and when you will be available
   B. write a short letter stating only that it is important that they contact you in order to arrange a meeting
   C. ask a secretary to help you because you do not really like to write to groups
   D. call the agency rather than write since you know someone there

   3.____

4. It is necessary for you to call the director of a head start center in order to discuss   4.____
   a training program for teaching aides. The operator asks who you are and
   what you wish to discuss with the director.
   Your response should be to
   A. tell her that you would rather explain to the director and you want to
      speak to her immediately
   B. identify yourself, your department, and the nature of your business with
      the director
   C. hang up and try to call again when another operator is on duty
   D. tell your supervisor that the operator at the head start center is rude and
      you would rather not be asked to call there again

5. Mr. A. wants her children to go to summer camp. She has receive the request   5.____
   forms, but does not understand all of the questions and you are asked to help
   her complete them. She comes to the office at the appointed time.
   Of the following, the action you should take is to
   A. tell her she has taken so long that maybe the children will not go to camp
   B. see her as quickly as possible, explain the questions to her, and help her
      in completing the forms
   C. help her, but tell her she will have to learn to read better and refer her to
      an evening school
   D. fill out the forms or her by yourself

6. Mrs. B. needs a referral to the cancer clinic. You contact the clinic and make   6.____
   arrangements for her visit. You go to her home to inform her about the time
   because she has no phone. She thanks you for your help and then offers you
   a piece of jewelry that appears to be rather expensive.
   Of the following, the action you should take is to
   A. take the gift because you don't want to hurt her feelings
   B. tell her that she is foolish and should spend her money on herself
   C. explain to her that you are pleased with her thoughtfulness, but you are
      unable to accept the gift
   D. refuse the gift and get someone else to make referrals in the future
      because she is trying to pay you for your help

7. Mrs. C., a seemingly healthy, intelligent woman whose husband is disabled, and   7.____
   who works part-time, asks for help in getting homemaker services.
   Of the following, the action you should take is to
   A. give Mrs. C. the necessary information and help her get the services
   B. tell Mrs. C. that you do not feel she needs these services since her
      husband is capable of helping
   C. make note of her request since you do not feel it is urgent
   D. refer her to a caseworker since she obviously needs help in defining her
      role as a woman

8. When you are interviewing clients, it is important to notice and record how they   8.____
   say what they say—angrily, nervously, or with "body English"—because these
   signs may

A. tell you that the client's words are the opposite of what the client feels and you may need to dig to find out what those feelings are
B. be the prelude to violent behavior which no aide is prepared to handle
C. show that the client does not really deserve serious consideration
D. be important later should you be asked to defend what you did for the client

9. You are recording a visit you have made with a client who was angry and abusive to you during the interview. At one point, you lost your temper and said some things that you immediately regretted. You are embarrassed to record that you lost your temper.
However, it would be desirable to record this MAINLY because
   A. you would feel guilty if you did not record it
   B. your supervisor might hear about it from the client, so it would be better to have it written down from your point of view
   C. your supervisor can use the information to help you to improve your skills
   D. it is agency policy to write down everything

10. Through one of your clients you learn that a day care program's hours have been extended. You confirm this information with the day care center.
It is then MOST important for you to
   A. make a note of this fact, since it will mean you have to change your schedule in working with the client
   B. add this information to your personal resource file so that you can refer other clients to the day dare program
   C. inform your supervisor of the new information so that it can be added to the central resource file
   D. ignore the information, since your client does not need to have her child in day care for any extra hours

11. You are sent to a meeting of day-care parents to explain the programs of your agency. One of the parents becomes very angry, saying that welfare departments treat people like animals.
You should remain as calm as possible and say to the parent that
   A. he is right, but you have no control over what your agency does
   B. he is disrupting the meeting and you have come to explain a program, not to listen to complaints
   C. you understand his feelings and that sometimes clients do not get the services they wish as quickly as possible; however, you will do whatever you can to assist him
   D. he should call your supervisor tomorrow and make an appointment to discuss his feelings

12. Assume that you receive a telephone call from a very angry father. His daughter took money from his wallet, and he wants the caseworker to control the daughter. He yells, screams, and swears at you.
What is the BEST way for you to respond?

A. Hang up because you are not responsible for his daughter's actions. He shouldn't scream and swear at you.
B. Remember to be courteous and polite at all times, never losing your temper
C. Transfer the call to the supervisor because you are concerned about the father's unreasonableness and do not want the responsibility of dealing with him
D. Tell him that behavior such as he is demonstrating is the reason his daughter steals from him

13. Mrs. D.'s son, aged 12, has been getting into difficulty in the neighborhood. At a community meeting, she asks your help in finding worthwhile activities for him. It is APPROPRIATE for you to respond to her because
    A. you should have knowledge of the social services available in the neighborhood and the activities they offer
    B. you have known Mrs. D. and her family for several years and know how much trouble she has had with her son
    C. it is your job to do what the caseworker assigns to you without question
    D. you are concerned about impressing Mrs. D with your knowledge

14. Several clients live in your neighborhood. They know that you work for the human resources administration. One day one of them tells you that there is a rumor that another client is pregnant and asks if this is true. You know from a past discussion with the caseworker that this client is pregnant.
    The BEST answer for you to give would be to
    A. tell her it is none of her business and if she wants to know, she should ask the caseworker
    B. ask her who told her that this client is pregnant
    C. explain that anything told to the agency is held in confidence and will not be shared with anyone else
    D. tell her you don't know, but will ask when you get back to the office and let her know later

15. The area senior citizens group asks for an agency representative to discuss old-age assistance and new SSI regulations. Your supervisor asks you to attend this meeting; however, you do not wish to go because you really do not feel that you work well with older people. In fact, you don't like them very much.
    What should be your response?
    A. Tell the supervisor that you cannot go because you have an appointment with the doctor that day
    B. Get another worker to go for you and assume his task while he is gone
    C. Explain to your supervisor what problems you have in working with old-age clients
    D. Go, because you should do the tasks that are assigned to you according to your job description

16. At a center where you are distributing literature about agency programs, a citizen comes up to you and begins to complain loudly about agency programs. What should be your response?   16._____
    A. Call the police and have the complainer removed from the center
    B. Tell him that you do not make policy; suggest that he go to the office and complain
    C. Remain as calm as possible and ask that he discuss the complaints with you calmly. If necessary, make an appointment with him
    D. Yell at him since this seems to be the way he relates to agency people

17. A community group is having a training program. You are sent to explain agency policy and answer questions.   17._____
    Providing this type of contact between the agency and community groups is PROPER because
    A. you like people and are a good public speaker
    B. it is the responsibility of the agency to cooperate with community groups in order to help the public to be well-informed about agency policy
    C. you were once in the same training program and understand the kind of people who are being trained
    D. once in a while everyone should have the opportunity to speak to a community group

18. While you are assisting in the intake area, a young man who is applying is cooperative but begins to ask you personal questions: your age, where you live, whether you have children, and other similar questions.   18._____
    You are disturbed by these questions, so you should
    A. tell him that agency policy does not allow you to answer personal questions and send him to another intake worker
    B. tell him it is your responsibility to ask questions, not his
    C. tell your supervisor that you do not want to work in intake because clients can get too nosy and you get nervous
    D. avoid answering personal questions and try to get him to return to the purpose of the interview

19. You are assigned to the reception area for the day. A mother arrives in the office with three small children. In a rage, she says that she does not have enough money to feed the children and demands that you find a home for them.   19._____
    The BEST action for you to take should be to
    A. call a security officer and have him remove her and the children from the office
    B. attempt to calm her down by listening to her, attend to the children's needs and call for a supervisor
    C. take the children from her and ask her to leave at once
    D. call the supervisor and security because it is their job to take care of abusive clients

20. Assume that you are interviewing a young unwed mother who has recently arrived in the city from Alabama. She is a likable girl and is very cooperative. However, it is difficult to understand the meaning of her conversation due to her accent and different use of words.
You would like to establish a good relationship with her, so you should FIRST
    A. suggest that she go to evening school so that she can learn to speak like other people in the city
    B. tell her that you don't understand her sometimes and you would appreciate it if she would explain what she means
    C. take another worker with you on visits to help you in the interview
    D. try to find a worker in the agency who has a similar background and have the case handled by the worker

21. A man being interviewed is entitled to Medicaid, but he refuses to sign up for it because he says he cannot accept any form of welfare.
Of the following, the BEST course of action for an aide to take FIRST is to
    A. try to discover the reason for his feeling this way
    B. tell him that he should be glad financial help is available
    C. explain that others cannot get help him if he will not help himself
    D. suggest that he speak to someone who is already on Medicaid

22. Of the following, the outcome of an interview by an aide depends MOS heavily on the
    A. personality of the interviewee
    B. personality of the aide
    C. subject matter of the questions asked
    D. interaction between aide and interviewee

23. Some patients being interviewed are PRIMARILY interested in making a favorable impression. The aide should be aware of the fact that such patients are more likely than other patients to
    A. try to anticipate the answers the interviewer is looking for
    B. answer all questions openly and frankly
    C. try to assume the role of interviewer
    D. be anxious to get the interview over as quickly as possible

24. The type of interview which an aide usually conducts is substantially different from most interviewing situations in all of the following aspects EXCEPT the
    A. setting   B. kinds of clients
    C. techniques employed D. kinds of problems

25. During an interview, an aide uses a "leading question."
This type of question is so-called because it generally
    A. starts a series of questions about one topic
    B. suggests the answer which the aide wants
    C. forms the basis for a following "trick" question
    D. sets, at the beginning, the tone of the interview

KEY (CORRECT ANSWERS)

1. C
2. C
3. A
4. B
5. B

6. C
7. A
8. A
9. C
10. C

11. C
12. B
13. A
14. C
15. C

16. C
17. B
18. D
19. B
20. B

21. A
22. D
23. A
24. C
25. B

TEST 2

DIRECTIONS: Each question or incomplete statement is followed by several suggested answers or completions. Select the one that BEST answers the question or completes the statement. *PRINT THE LETTER OF THE CORRECT ANSWER IN THE SPACE AT THE RIGHT.*

1. Miss Lally is an old-age assistance recipient. Her health is not good and it is important that she have three good meals each day. She follows these instructions except on Friday she refuses to eat meat because of her religious beliefs. She will not even substitute fish.
   You are very concerned about this, so you should
   A. tell your supervisor so that she will go to see Miss Lally and make her eat nourishing meals on Friday
   B. call her doctor and tell him so that he will see her and explain to her that fasting is not good for her health
   C. attempt to understand her value system and accept that it is possible that she is acting in good faith with her own values even though they may be harmful to her health
   D. explain to her how important it is that she eat meat each day in order to be in good health and enjoy the remaining years of her life

2. Theodore is a junkie. Every cent he can get his hands on legally or illegally is used to supply his habit. You are angry because the junkie is destroying himself and his family. You feel that the courts should punish him for his illegal acts.
   Of the following, the BEST action for you to take is to
   A. suggest to your supervisor that the income maintenance center reduce the family grant, taking out his portion
   B. help his wife to find another apartment for her and the children away from him
   C. call the local police to find out why they are doing nothing about this man's activities in the community
   D. reconsider your ideas about punishment, remembering that punishment alone will not help the man to change his behavior

3. You are regularly assigned to taking Sarah Jones and her young son to the clinic. She is a very warm, friendly woman and your relationship with her is good. However, she invited you to come for dinner on Sunday and to go to a school play with her. You would like to accept the invitations because you need weekend activities and you like her.
   What should be your PRIMARY consideration in coming to a decision?
   A. You need friends just as she does, so you should accept the invitations
   B. You are a worker and should not be seen with a client in public places
   C. Decide whether accepting the invitations will help to meet agency needs or will hamper the relationship you are expected to establish
   D. Tell her "no" because it is not a good policy to be on such friendly terms with clients

4. Martha's husband has been arrested in a drug raid and she is extremely anxious. Your supervisor asks that you visit her to determine ways in which the agency may help her. You visit and find her weeping; the house and the children have obviously been neglected.
The BEST thing for you to do is to
   A. tell her to stop crying and help her to clean the apartment and the children
   B. remind her that her husband has been warned and now has to pay for not listening
   C. listen to her, allowing her to express her feelings of fear, loss, and grief, and reassure her of your concern
   D. listen to her but caution her that she is neglecting the home and children because of her anxiety and you may have to ask your supervisor to remove the children if she doesn't get any better

5. Mrs. Dwight's landlord is very slow in making repairs in her apartment. Each time you see her, she complains about this over and over again, calling her landlord names and threatening to report him to the city. She complains to any agency person she meets.
Realizing that these complaints are not getting any action, you should
   A. avoid meeting with her because she is annoying
   B. suggest that she see a doctor because she is irrational and should get some help
   C. ask her what she would like to do about the problem and assist her in carrying out her plans
   D. ask the supervisor to see her because you do not have the skills to help her

6. In the day-to-day operations of the human resources administration, which of the following would you consider to be the PRIMARY function of the agency?
   A. Getting work done to meet city and federal deadlines
   B. Being sure that all of the clients who come to the agency are seen before closing time
   C. Delivering services to those persons who are eligible for assistance
   D. Making sure everyone gets his check on time

7. During the course of an interview you find it is necessary to arrange a special appointment for the client to return for a further interview. After checking your calendar, you tell the client the date she is to come back. The client, however, says she cannot see you on that date because she is to attend a rally at a community center in her neighborhood.
Of the following, your BEST action should be to
   A. let her know that any other day is an inconvenience to you and remind her that the appointment is for her benefit
   B. forget about the special appointment and try to get along with the information you have
   C. explain to her the need for the appointment and ask when she can meet with you
   D. tell her that since the community center is not city-operated, she must keep her appointment with you

8. In working with community groups, it is important that you be able to define what a community is.
   Of the following definitions, which is the MOST appropriate?
   A community
   A. consists of a group of people living fairly close together in a more or less compact territory, who come together in their chief concerns
   B. is a particular section of a city designated on a census tract
   C. is that portion of a city which constitutes an election district
   D. is a section of a city or town in which a particular ethnic group conducts its social, business, and religious life

9. The agency has implemented a new policy regarding the intake procedure. You wish to explain and discuss this policy with as many community groups as possible. You make an initial contact by mail.
   In order to get your message across well, your letter should be
   A. short and as concise as possible explaining why you want to meet with them, and offer several possible times that you will be available
   B. short, explaining only that it is important that the groups contact you in order to arrange a meeting
   C. drafted by the center's secretary and sent to the usual groups
   D. put in the usual announcement form in the center's newsletter

10. A group of young welfare mothers want to form an organization that will provide babysitting services for mothers of children who are too young to enroll in a day care center.
    What should be your answer to them?
    A. Tell them to try to get the center to change its policy to include young children
    B. Arrange the time to meet with them to offer as much advice and support as possible, since most communities do need this service
    C. Suggest that it may be better that they spend their time taking care of their own children
    D. Ask a social worker to survey the community to determine if such a service is really needed at this time

11. New regulations have removed the disabled, blind, and old-age assistance cases from the public assistance caseload. Assistance in these categories is given directly by the federal government. A former client has not received his check. The chairman of the senior citizens committee calls and angrily demands that your agency do something in this man's behalf.
    In response, you should
    A. answer politely, explaining that your agency is not concerned about OAA clients
    B. arrange to meet with him in order to discuss the new policy
    C. refer him to the Social Security office covering the area where the client lives
    D. ask that he call again when he is calmer so that you may discuss this matter with him

12. A high school student from the community comes to see you about a homework assignment to write a report on your center.
    The BEST way to help him is to
    A. refer him to a social worker who has daily contact with clients in their homes
    B. contact the boy's teacher and find out why you were not warned of his coming
    C. explain your center's program and answer as many of his questions as you can
    D. give him literature about the welfare system in the city and state

13. Assume that the women's group of the Community Baptist Church has invited you to a Sunday afternoon service to celebrate the tenth anniversary of the pastor. The agency's relationship with the women is good in that they often offer their homes as emergency homes for adult clients.
    What should you do about the invitation?
    A. Do not attend but send them a note congratulating the pastor and explaining that agency personnel do not work on Sundays
    B. Ask a social worker who lives close to the church to go
    C. Accept the invitation if at all possible, attend the service and whatever social hour they may have afterwards
    D. Ignore the invitation since this function has little relationship to your job

14. Suppose that a person you are interviewing becomes angry at some of the questions you have asked, calls you meddlesome and nosy, and states that she will not answer those questions.
    Of the following, which is the BEST action for you to take
    A. Explain the reasons the questions are asked and the importance of the answers
    B. Inform the interviewee that you are only doing your job and advise her that she should answer your questions or leave your office
    C. Report to your supervisor what the interviewee called you and refuse to continue the interview
    D. End the interview and tell the interviewee she will not be serviced by your department

15. Suppose that during the course of an interview the interviewee demands in a very rude way that she be permitted to talk to your supervisor or someone in charge.
    Which of the following is probably the BEST way to handle this situation?
    A. Inform your supervisor of the demand and ask her to speak to the interviewee
    B. Pay no attention to the demands of the interviewee and continue the interview
    C. Report to your supervisor and tell her to get another interviewer for this interviewee
    D. Tell her you are the one "in charge" and that she should talk to you

16. Suppose that a worker asks a client to answer several required but rather personal questions about the family's health history. The client delays and seems embarrassed about giving the answers.
    Of the following, the MOST reasonable response to the client is one which
    A. shows an awareness of the client's efforts to hide something
    B. demonstrates the worker's qualifications for asking such questions
    C. allows this client to be excused from answering the questions
    D. convinces the client that his uneasiness in the situation is understood

17. A representative from a planned parenthood group comes to see you to get information for a community education program.
    You should
    A. check out this group to make sure it is not promoting zero population growth for minority groups
    B. develop a good relationship with him so as to provide better service to clients
    C. make sure they will not encourage unnecessary abortions
    D. refuse to see him

18. A member of a clerical training program is continually late to classes. He explains to you that he has a hard time getting up and asks that you report him on time because he needs to train for a job.
    What should your response be?
    A. Tell him that you get there on time and so should he
    B. Tell him that you do not lie for anyone
    C. Explain that it is your duty to keep accurate records and refer him to a counselor
    D. Tell him that you will cooperate with him but he has to try to do better

19. In a community meeting to explain a new agency policy, you find that the audience has no questions about the policy or your explanations.
    What would be the MOST appropriate response to the silence?
    A. Leave right away before they think of questions
    B. Thank the audience for their attention and assure them that you will be available if there are any questions later
    C. Ask several members in the audience if they understand the new policy
    D. Explain that the audience could not possibly understand all of the policy and they must have questions

20. Assume that you are confronted by an angry member of the public who has not been able to obtain the information he needs from your office. You do not know the answer to his question.
    The BEST thing for you to do would be to
    A. tell him to come back another time, after you have looked up the information
    B. check with your supervisor to find the correct answer

C. tell him to ask in another office, so that you will not lose time looking for the information
D. make up and answer to keep the man satisfied until the right answer is found

KEY (CORRECT ANSWERS)

1.	C	11.	C
2.	D	12.	C
3.	C	13.	C
4.	C	14.	A
5.	C	15.	A
6.	C	16.	D
7.	C	17.	B
8.	A	18.	C
9.	A	19.	B
10.	B	20.	B

EXAMINATION SECTION
TEST 1

DIRECTIONS: Each question or incomplete statement is followed by several suggested answers or completions. Select the one that BEST answers the question or completes the statement. *PRINT THE LETTER OF THE CORRECT ANSWER IN THE SPACE AT THE RIGHT.*

1. When a worker is planning a future interview with a client, of the following, the MOST important consideration is the
   A. recommendations he will make to the client
   B. place where the client will be interviewed
   C. purpose for which the client will be interviewed
   D. personality of the client

2. For a worker to make a practice of reviewing the client's case record, if available, prior to the interview is usually
   A. *inadvisable*, because knowledge of the client's past record will tend to influence the worker's judgment
   B. *advisable*, because knowledge of the client's background will help the worker to identify discrepancies in the client's responses
   C. *inadvisable*, because such review is time-consuming and of questionable value
   D. *advisable*, because knowledge of the client's background will help the worker to understand the client's situation

3. Assume that a worker makes a practice of constantly re-assuring clients with serious and complex problems by making such statements as: *I'm sure you'll soon be well; I know you'll get a job soon*; or *Everything will be all right*.
   Of the following, the MOST likely result of such practice is to
   A. encourage the client and make him feel that the worker understands what the client is going through
   B. make the client doubtful about the worker's understanding of his difficulties and the worker's ability to help
   C. confuse the client and cause him to hesitate to take any action on his own initiative
   D. help the client to be more realistic about his situation and the probability that it will improve

4. In order to get the maximum amount of information from a client during an interview, of the following, it is MOST important for the worker to communicate to the client the feeling that the worker is
   A. interested in the client
   B. a figure of authority
   C. efficient in his work habits
   D. sympathetic to the client's lifestyle

5. Of the following, the worker who takes extremely detailed notes during an interview with a client is MOST likely to
   A. encourage the client to talk freely
   B. distract and antagonize the client
   C. help the client feel at ease
   D. understand the client's feelings

6. You find that many of the clients you interview are verbally abusive and unusually hostile to you.
   Of the following, the MOST appropriate action for you to take FIRST is to
   A. review your interviewing techniques and consider whether you may be provoking these clients
   B. act in a more authoritative manner when interviewing troublesome clients
   C. tell these clients that you will not process their applications unless their troublesome behavior ceases
   D. disregard the clients' troublesome behavior during the interviews

7. During an interview, you did not completely understand several of your client's responses. In each instance, you rephrased the client's statement and asked the client if that was what he meant.
   For you to use such a technique during interviews would be considered
   A. *inappropriate*; you may have distorted the client's meaning by rephrasing his statements
   B. *inappropriate*; you should have asked the same question until you received a comprehensible response
   C. *appropriate*; the client will have a chance to correct you if you have misinterpreted his responses
   D. *appropriate*; a worker should rephrase clients' responses for the records

8. A worker is interviewing a client who has just had a severe emotional shock because of an assault on her by a mugger.
   Of the following, the approach which would generally be MOST helpful to the client is for the worker to
   A. comfort the client and encourage her to talk about the assault
   B. sympathize with the client but refuse to talk about the assault
   C. tell the client to control her emotions and think positively about the future
   D. proceed with the interview in an impersonal and unemotional manner

9. A worker finds that her questions are misinterpreted by many of the clients she interviews.
   Of the following, the MOST likely reason for this problem is that the
   A. client is not listening attentively
   B. client wants to avoid the subject being discussed
   C. worker has failed to express her meaning clearly
   D. worker has failed to put the client at ease

10. For a worker to look directly at the client and observe him during the interview is, generally,
    A. *inadvisable*; this will make the client nervous and uncomfortable
    B. *advisable*; the client will be more likely to refrain from lying
    C. *inadvisable*; the worker will not be able to take notes for the case record
    D. *advisable*; this will encourage conversation and accelerate the progress of the interview

11. You are interviewing a client who is applying for social services for the first time. In order to encourage this client to freely give you the information needed for you to establish his eligibility, of the following, the BEST way to start the interview is by
    A. asking questions the client can easily answer
    B. conveying the impression that his responses to your questions will be checked
    C. asking two or three similar but important questions
    D. assuring the client that your sole responsibility is *getting the facts*

12. Workers are encouraged to record significant information obtained from clients and services provided for clients.
    Of the following, the MOST important reason for this practice is that these case records will
    A. help to reduce the need for regular supervisory conferences
    B. indicate to workers which clients are taking up the most time
    C. provide information which will help the agency to improve its services to clients
    D. make it easier to verify the complaints of clients

13. As a worker in the employment eligibility section, you find that interviews can be completed in a shorter period of time if you ask questions which limit the client to a certain answer.
    For you to use such a technique would be considered
    A. *inappropriate*, because this type of question usually requires advance preparation
    B. *inappropriate*, because this type of question may inhibit the client from saying what he really means
    C. *appropriate*, because you know the areas into which the questions should be directed
    D. *appropriate*, because this type of question usually helps clients to express themselves clearly

14. Assume that a worker at a juvenile detention center is planning foster care placement for a child.
    For the worker to have the child participate in the planning is generally considered to be
    A. time-consuming and of little practical value in preparing the child for placement
    B. valuable in helping the child adjust to future placement

C. useful, because the child will be more likely to cooperate with others in the center
D. anxiety-provoking because the child will feel that he has been abandoned

15. You have been assigned to interview the mother of a five-year-old son in her home to get information useful in locating the child's absent father. During the interview, you notice many serious bruises on the child's arms and legs, which the mother explains are due to the child's clumsiness.
Of the following, your BEST course of action is to
   A. accept the mother's explanation and concentrate on getting information which will help you to locate the father
   B. advise the mother to have the child examined for a medical condition that may be causing his clumsiness
   C. make a surprise visit to the mother later, to see whether someone is beating the child
   D. complete your interview with the mother and report the case to your supervisor for investigation of possible child abuse

15.____

16. During an interview, the former landlord of an absent father offers to help you to locate the father if you will give the landlord confidential information you have on the financial situation of the father.
Of the following, you should
   A. immediately end the interview with the landlord
   B. urge the landlord to help you but explain that you are not permitted to give him confidential information
   C. freely give the landlord the confidential information he requests about the father
   D. give the landlord the information only if he promises to keep it confidential

16.____

17. You feel that your client, a released mental patient, is not adjusting well to living on his own in an apartment. To gather more information, you interview privately his next-door neighbor, who claims that the client is creating a disturbance and speaks of the client in an angry and insulting manner.
Of the following, the BEST action for you to take in this situation is to
   A. listen patiently to the neighbor to try to get the facts about your client's behavior
   B. inform the neighbor that he has no right to speak insultingly about a mentally ill person
   C. make an appointment to interview the neighbor some other time when he isn't so upset
   D. tell the neighbor that you were not aware of the client's behavior and that you will have the client moved

17.____

18. As a worker assigned to an income maintenance center, you are interviewing a client to determine his eligibility for a work program. Suddenly, the client begins to shout that he is in no condition to work and that you are persecuting him for no reason.

18.____

Of the following, your BEST response to this client is to
- A. advise the client to stop shouting or you will call for the security guard
- B. wait until the client calms down, then order him to come back for another interview
- C. insist that you are not persecuting the client and that he must complete the interview
- D. wait until the client calms down, say that you understand how he feels, and try to continue the interview

19. You are counseling a mother whose 17-year-old son has recently been returned home from a mental institution. Although she is willing to care for her son at home, she is frightened by his strange and sometimes violent behavior and does not know the best arrangement to make for his care.
Of the following, your MOST appropriate response to this mother's problem is to
    - A. describe the supportive services and alternatives to home care which are available
    - B. help her to accept her son's strange and violent behavior
    - C. tell her that she will not be permitted to care for her son at home if she is frightened by his behavior
    - D. convince her that she is not responsible for her son's mental condition

20. Assume that, as an intake worker, you are interviewing an elderly man who comes to the center several times a month to discuss topics with you which are not related to social service. You realize that the man is lonely and enjoys these conversations.
Of the following, it would be MOST appropriate to
    - A. politely discourage the man from coming in to pass the time with you
    - B. avoid speaking to this man the next time he comes into the center
    - C. explore with the client his feelings about joining a Senior Citizens' Center
    - D. continue to hold these conversations with the man

21. A client you are interviewing in the housing elibility section tends to ramble on after each response that he gives, so that man clients are kept waiting.
In this situation, of the following, it would be MOST advisable to
    - A. try to direct the interview, in order to obtain the necessary information
    - B. reduce the number of questions asked so that you can shorten the interview
    - C. arrange a second interview for the client so that you can give him more time
    - D. tell the client that he is wasting everybody's time

22. A non-minority worker in an employment eligibility unit is about to interview a minority client on public assistance for job placement when the client says:
What does your kind know about my problems? You've never had to survive out on these streets.
Of the following, the worker's MOST appropriate response to this situation is to

A. postpone the interview until a minority worker is available to interview the client
B. tell the client that he must cooperate with the worker if he wants to continue receiving public assistance
C. explain to the client the function of the worker in this unit and the services he provides
D. assure the client that you do not have to be a member of a minority group to understand the effects of poverty

23. As a worker in a family services unit, you have been assigned to follow-up a case folder recently forwarded from the protective-diagnostic unit.
After making appropriate clerical notations in your records such as name of client and date of receipt, which of the following would be the MOST appropriate step to take next?
    A. Confer with your supervisor
    B. Read and review all reports included in the case folder
    C. Arrange to visit with the client at his home
    D. Confer with representatives of any other agencies which have been in contact with the client

24. As a worker in the employment section, you are interviewing a young client who seriously underestimates the amount of education and training he will require for a certain occupation.
For you to tell the client that you think he is mistaken would, generally, be considered
    A. *inadvisable*, because workers should not express their opinions to clients
    B. *inadvisable*, because clients have the right to self-determination
    C. *advisable*, because clients should generally be alerted to their misconceptions
    D. *advisable*, because workers should convince clients to adopt a proper lifestyle

25. As an intake worker, you are counseling a mother and her unmarried, thirteen-year-old daughter, who is six months pregnant, concerning the advisability of placing the daughter's baby for adoption. The mother insists on adoption, but the daughter remains silent and appears undecided.
Of the following, you should encourage the daughter to
    A. make the final decision on adoption herself
    B. keep her baby despite her mother's insistence on adoption
    C. accept her mother's insistence on adoption
    D. make the decision on adoption together with her mother

KEY (CORRECT ANSWERS)

1. C
2. D
3. B
4. A
5. B

6. A
7. C
8. A
9. C
10. D

11. A
12. C
13. B
14. B
15. D

16. B
17. A
18. D
19. A
20. C

21. A
22. C
23. B
24. C
25. D

TEST 2

DIRECTIONS: Each question or incomplete statement is followed by several suggested answers or completions. Select the one that BEST answers the question or completes the statement. *PRINT THE LETTER OF THE CORRECT ANSWER IN THE SPACE AT THE RIGHT.*

1. You are interviewing a legally responsible absent father who refuses to make child support payments because he claims the mother physically abuses the child.
   Of the following, the BEST way for you to handle his situation is to tell the father that you
   A. will report his complaint about the mother, but he is still responsible for making child support payments
   B. suspect that he is complaining about the mother in order to avoid his own responsibility for making child support payments
   C. are concerned with his responsibility to make child support payments, not with the mother's abuse of the child
   D. cannot determine his responsibility for making child support payments until his complaint about the mother is investigated

   1.____

2. On a visit to a home where child abuse is alleged, you find the mother preparing lunch for her two children. She tells you that she knows that a neighbor is spreading lies about her treatment of the children.
   Which one of the following is the BEST action for you to take?
   A. Thank the mother for her assistance, leave the home, and indicate in your report that the allegation of child abuse is false
   B. Tell the mother that, since you have been sent to visit her, there must be some truth to the allegations
   C. Explain the purpose of your visit and observe whatever interaction takes place between the children and the mother
   D. Conclude the interview, since you have observed the mother preparing a good lunch for the children

   2.____

3. You are interviewing an elderly woman who lives alone to determine her eligibility for homemaker service at public expense. Though obviously frail and in need of this service, the woman is not completely cooperative, and, during the interview, is often silent for a considerable period of time.
   Of the following, the BEST way for you to deal with these periods of silence is to
   A. realize that she may be embarrassed to have to apply for homemaker service at public expense, and emphasize her right to this service
   B. postpone the interview and make an appointment with her for a later date, when she may be better able to cooperate
   C. explain to the woman that you have many clients to interview and need her cooperation to complete the interview quickly
   D. recognize that she is probably hiding something and begin to ask questions to draw her out

   3.____

2 (#2)

4. During a conference with an adolescent boy at a juvenile detention center, you find out for the first time that he would prefer to be placed in foster care rather than return to his natural parents.
To uncover the reasons why the boy dislikes his own home, of the following, it would be MOST advisable for you to
   A. ask the boy a number of short, simple questions about his feelings
   B. encourage the boy to talk freely and express his feelings as best he can
   C. interview the parents and find out why the boy doesn't want to live at home
   D. administer a battery of psychological tests in order to make an assessment of the boy's problems

1._____

5. Of the following, the BEST way to determine which activities should be provided for members of a Senior Citizens' Center is to
   A. ask the neighborhood community board to submit their recommendations
   B. meet with the professional staff of the center to get their opinions
   C. encourage the members of the center to express their personal preferences
   D. study the schedules prepared by other Senior Citizens' Centers for guidance

5._____

6. You are interviewing a mother who is applying for Aid to Families with Dependent Children because the husband has deserted the family. The mother becomes annoyed at having to answer your questions and tells you to leave her apartment.
Which one of the following actions would be MOST appropriate to take FIRST in this situation?
   A. Return to the office and close the case for lack of cooperation
   B. Tell the mother that you will get the information from her neighbors if she does not cooperate
   C. Tell the mother that you must stay until you get answers to your questions
   D. Explain to the mother the reasons for the interview and the consequences of her failure to cooperate

6._____

7. A worker assigned to visit homebound clients to determine their eligibility for Medicaid must understand each client's situation as completely as possible.
Of the following source which may provide insight into the client's situation, the one that is generally MOST revealing is:
   A. Close relatives of the client, who have known him for many years
   B. Next-door neighbors, who have observed the daily living habits of the client
   C. The client himself, who can provide his own description of his situation
   D. The records of other social agencies that may have served the client

7._____

8. A worker counseling juvenile clients finds that, although he can tolerate most of their behavior, he becomes infuriated when they lie to him.
Of the following, the worker can BEST deal with his anger at his clients' lying by

8._____

61

A. recognizing his feelings of anger and learning to control expression of these feelings to his clients
B. warning his clients that he cannot be responsible for his anger when a client lies to him
C. using willpower to suppress his feelings of anger when a client lies to him
D. realizing that lying is a common trait of juveniles and not directed against him personally

9. During an interview at the employment eligibility section, one of your clients, a former drug addict, has expressed an interest in attending a community counseling center and resuming his education.
In this case, the MOST appropriate action that you should take FIRST is to
A. determine whether this ambition is realistic for a former drug addict
B. send the client's application to a community counseling center which provides services to former addicts
C. ask the client whether he is really motivated or is just seeking your approval
D. encourage and assist the client to take this step, since his interest is a positive sign

9.____

10. Because of habitual neglect by his mother, a five-year-old boy has been placed in a foster home.
For the worker to encourage the mother to visit the boy in the foster home is, generally,
A. *desirable*, because the boy will be helped by continuing his ties with his mother
B. *undesirable*, because the boy will be upset by his mother's visits and will have a harder time adjusting to the foster home
C. *desirable*, because the mother will learn from the foster parents how she should treat the boy
D. *undesirable*, because the mother should be punished for her neglect of the boy by complete separation from him

10.____

11. You are interviewing a client who, during previous appointments, has not responded to your requests for information required to determine his continued eligibility for services. On this occasion, the client again offers an excuse which you feel is not acceptable.
For you to advise the client of the probable loss of services because of his lack of cooperation is
A. *inappropriate*, because the threat to withhold services will harm the relationship between worker and client
B. *inappropriate*, because workers should not reveal to clients that they do not believe their statements
C. *appropriate*, because social services are a reward given to cooperative clients
D. *appropriate*, because the worker should inform clients of the consequences of their lack of cooperation

11.____

4 (#2)

12. Assume that you are counseling an adolescent boy in a juvenile detention center who has been a ringleader in smuggling pot into the center.
During your regular interview with this boy, of the following, it would be *advisable* to
    A. tell him you know that he has been involved in smuggling pot and that you are trying to understand the reasons for his misbehavior
    B. ignore his pot smuggling in order to reassure him that you understand and accept him, even though you do not agree with his standards of behavior
    C. warn him that you have reported his pot smuggling and that he will be punished for his misbehavior
    D. show him that you disagree of his pot smuggling, but assure him that you will not report him for his misbehavior

12.____

13. Your unit has received several complaints about a homeless elderly woman living outdoors in various locations in the area. To help determine the need for protective services for this woman, you interview several persons in the neighborhood who are familiar with her, but all are uncooperative or reluctant to give information.
Of the following, your BEST approach to these persons is to explain to them that
    A. you will take legal steps against them if they do not cooperate with you
    B. their cooperation may enable you to help this homeless woman
    C. you need their cooperation to remove this homeless woman from their neighborhood
    D. they will be responsible for any harm that comes to this homeless woman

13.____

14. A foster mother complains to the worker that a ten-year-old boy placed with her is overaggressive and unmanageable. The worker, knowing that the boy has been placed unsuccessfully several times before, constantly reassures the foster mother that the boy is improving steadily.
For the worker to do this, generally,
    A. *good practice*, because the foster mother may accept the professional opinion of the worker and keep the boy
    B. *poor practice*, because the foster mother may be discouraged from discussing the boy's problems with the worker
    C. *good practice*, because the foster mother may feel guilty if she gives up the boy when he is improving
    D. *poor practice*, because the boy should not remain with a foster mother who complains about his behavior

14.____

15. Assume that, as a worker in the liaison and adjustment unit, you are interviewing a client regarding an adjustment in budget. The client begins to scream at you that she holds you responsible for the decrease in her allowance.
Of the following, which is the BEST way for you to handle this situation?
    A. Attempt to discuss the matter calmly with the client and explain her right to a hearing
    B. Urge the client to appeal and assure her of your support

15.____

C. Tell the client that her disorderly behavior will be held against her
D. Tell the client that the reduction is due to red tape and is not your fault

16. As a worker assigned to a juvenile detention center, you are having a counseling interview with a recently admitted boy who is having serious problems in adjusting to confinement in the center. During the interview, the boy frequently interrupts to ask you personal questions.
Of the following, the BEST way for you to deal with these questions is to
    A. tell him in a friendly way that your job is to discuss his problems, not yours
    B. try to understand how the questions relate to the boy's own problems and reply with discretion
    C. take no notice of the questions and continue with the interview
    D. try to win the boy's confidence by answering his questions in detail

17. A worker is interviewing an elderly woman who hesitates to provide necessary information about her finances to determine whether she is eligible for supplementary assistance. She fears that this information will be reported to others and that her neighbors will find out that she is destitute and applying for welfare.
Of the following, the worker's MOST appropriate response is to
    A. tell her that, if she hesitates to give this information, the agency will get it from other sources
    B. assure her that this information is kept strictly confidential, and will not be given to unauthorized persons
    C. convince her that her application will be turned down unless she provides this information as soon as possible
    D. ask for the name and address of her nearest relative and obtain the information from that person

18. You are counseling a couple whose children have been placed in a foster home because of the couple's quarrelling and child neglect. When you interview the wife by herself, she tells you that she knows the husband often cheats on her with other women, but she is too afraid of the husband's temper to tell him how much this hurts her.
For you to immediately reveal to the husband the wife's unhappiness concerning his cheating is, generally,
    A. *good practice*, because it will help the husband to understand why his wife quarrels with him
    B. *poor practice*, because information received from the wife should not be given to the husband without her permission
    C. *good practice*, because the husband will direct his anger at you rather than at his wife
    D. *poor practice*, because the wife may have told you a false story about her husband in order to win your sympathy

6 (#2)

19. A worker in an employment eligibility section is beginning a job placement interview with a tall, strongly-built young man. As the man sits down, the worker comments: *I know a big fellow like you wouldn't be interested in any clerical job.*
    For the worker to make such a comment is, generally,
    A. *appropriate*, because it creates an air of familiarity which may put the man at ease
    B. *inappropriate*, because the man may be sensitive about his physical size
    C. *appropriate*, because the worker is using his judgment to help speed up the interview
    D. *inappropriate*, because the man may feel he is being pressured into agreeing with the worker

19.____

20. Workers at a juvenile detention center are responsible for establishing constructive relationships with the youths confined to the center in order to help them adjust to detention.
    Of the following, the BEST way for a worker to deal with a youth who acts over-aggressive and hostile is to
    A. take appropriate disciplinary measures
    B. attempt to distract the youth by encouraging him to engage in physical sports
    C. try to discover the real reasons for the youth's hostile behavior
    D. urge the youth to express his anger against the institution instead of *taking it out* on you

20.____

21. A worker in a men's shelter is counseling a middle-aged client for alcoholism. During counseling, the client confesses that, many years ago, he had often enjoyed sexually abusing his ten-year-old daughter. The worker tells the client that he personally finds the client's behavior *morally disgusting.*
    For the worker to tell the client this is, generally,
    A. *acceptable counseling practice*, because it may encourage the client to feel guilty about his behavior
    B. *unacceptable counseling practice*, because the client may try to shock the worker by confessing other similar behavior
    C. *acceptable counseling practice*, because *letting off steam* in this manner may relieve tension between the worker and the client
    D. *unacceptable counseling practice*, because the client may hesitate to discuss his behavior frankly with the worker in the future

21.____

22. During your discussion with a foster mother who has had a nine-year-old boy in placement for about one month, you are told that the child is disruptive in school and has been unruly and hostile toward the foster family. The boy had been quiet and docile before placement.
    In this situation, it would be MOST appropriate to suggest to the foster mother that
    A. this behavior is normal for a nine-year-old boy
    B. children placed in foster homes usually go through a period of testing their foster parents

22.____

C. the child must have picked up these patterns from the foster family
D. this behavior is probably a sign that she is too strict with the boy

23. During an interview in the housing eligibility section, your client, who wants to move to a larger apartment, asks you to decide on a suitable neighborhood for her.
For you, the worker, to make such a decision for the client would generally be considered
    A. *appropriate*, because you can save time and expense by sharing your knowledge of neighborhoods with the client
    B. *inappropriate*, because workers should not help clients with this type of decision
    C. *appropriate*, because this will help the client to develop confidence in her ability to make decisions
    D. *inappropriate*, because the client should be encouraged to accept the responsibility of making this decision

24. Your client, an elderly man left unable to care for himself after a stroke, has been referred for home-attendant services, but insists that he does not need these services. You believe that the man considers this to be an insult to his pride and that he will not allow himself to admit that he needs help.
Of the following, the MOST appropriate action for you to take is to
    A. withdraw the referral for home-attendant services and allow the client to try to take care of himself
    B. process the request for home-attendant services on the assumption that the client will soon realize that he cannot care for himself
    C. discuss with the client your interpretation of his problem and attempt to persuade him to accept home-attendant services
    D. tell the client that he will have no further opportunity to apply for home-attendant services if he does not accept them at this time

25. A worker making a field visit to investigate a complaint of child abuse finds that the parents of the child are a racially mixed couple. The child appears poorly dressed and unruly.
Of the following, the MOST appropriate approach for the worker to take in this situation is to
    A. take the child aside and ask him privately if either of his parents ever mistreats him
    B. determine if prejudice against the couple has led them to use the child as a scapegoat
    C. question the non-minority parent closely for signs of resentment of the child's mixed parentage
    D. observe the relationship between parents and child for indications of abuse by the parents

KEY (CORRECT ANSWERS)

1.	A	11.	D
2.	C	12.	A
3.	A	13.	B
4.	B	14.	B
5.	C	15.	A
6.	D	16.	B
7.	C	17.	B
8.	A	18.	B
9.	D	19.	D
10.	A	20.	C

21. D
22. B
23. D
24. C
25. D

EXAMINATION SECTION
TEST 1

DIRECTIONS: Each question or incomplete statement is followed by several suggested answers or completions. Select the one that BEST answers the question or completes the statement. *PRINT THE LETTER OF THE CORRECT ANSWER IN THE SPACE AT THE RIGHT.*

1. A client tells you that he is extremely upset by the treatment that he received from Center personnel at the information desk.
   Which of the following is the BEST way to handle this complaint during the interview?
   A. Explain to the client that he probably misinterpreted what occurred at the information desk
   B. Let the client express his feelings and then proceed with the interview
   C. Tell the client that you are not concerned with the personnel at the information desk
   D. Escort the client to the information desk to find out what really happened

2. As a worker in the foster home division, you are reviewing a case record to determine whether a 13-year-old boy, in foster care because of neglect and mistreatment by his natural parents, should be returned home. The natural parents, who want to take the child back, have been in family counseling, with encouraging result, and have improved their living conditions.
   Of the following, it would be appropriate to recommend that the child
   A. remain with the foster parents, since this is a documented case of child abuse
   B. remain with the foster parents until they are ready to send him home
   C. be returned to his natural parents, since they have made positive efforts to change their behavior toward the child
   D. be returned to his natural parents, because continued separation will cause irreparable damage to the child

3. You are finishing an interview with a client in which you have explained to her the procedure she must go through to apply for income maintenance.
   Of the following, the BEST way for you to make sure that she has fully understood the procedure is too ask her
   A. whether she feels she has understood your explanation of the procedure
   B. whether she has any questions to ask you about the procedure
   C. to describe the procedure to you in her own words
   D. a few questions to test her understanding of the procedure

4. Mrs. Carey, a widow with five children, has come to the field office to seek foster care for her 13-year-old daughter, who has often been truant from school and has recently been caught shoplifting. Mrs. Carey says that she cannot maintain a proper home environment for the other four children and deal with her daughter at the same time.

Of the following, you should FIRST
- A. process Mrs. Carey's request for placement of her daughter in a foster care agency
- B. interview both Mrs. Carey and her daughter to get a more complete picture of the situation
- C. suggest to Mrs. Care that she might be able to manage if she obtained homemaker services
- D. warn the daughter that she will be sent away from home if she does not change her behavior

5. During a group orientation meeting with couples who wish to adopt babies through your agency, one couple asks you how they should deal with the question of whether the child should be told that he is adopted.
Of the following, your BEST response to this couple is to
- A. tell them to conceal from the child the fact that he is adopted
- B. suggest that they lead the child to believe that his natural parents are dead
- C. tell them to inform the child that they know nothing about his natural parents
- D. explore with them their feelings about revealing to the child that he is adopted

6. You are beginning an investigation of an anonymous complaint that a welfare client has a concealed bank account.
Of the following, the FIRST step you should generally take in conducting this investigation is to
- A. confront the client with the complaint during an office interview
- B. try to track down the source of the anonymous complaint
- C. make a surprise visit to the client in his home to question him
- D. gather any available information from bank and agency records

7. When investigating the location of an absent parent, the worker frequently interviews the parent's friends and neighbors. The worker often writes down the information given by the person interviewed and, at the end of the interview, summarizes the information to the person.
For the worker to do this is, generally,
- A. *good practice*, because the person interviewed will be impressed by the efficiency of the worker
- B. *poor practice*, because the person interviewed may become impatient with the worker for repeating the information
- C. *good practice*, because the person interviewed has an opportunity to correct any errors the worker may have in recording the information
- D. *poor practice*, because summarizing the information may encourage the person to waste time adding and changing information

8. During an interview for the purpose of investigating a charge of child abuse, a client first denied that she had abused her child, but then burst into tears and promised that she *will never do it again*.
   Of the following, the MOST appropriate action for the worker to take in this situation is to
   A. tell the client that, since she has already lied, it is difficult to believe that she will keep her promise
   B. show a concern for the client's feelings but tell her that you will have to report your findings and refer her for help
   C. determine the extent to which the child was abused and close the case if no permanent harm was done
   D. explain to the client that she has already done enough harm to the child and you must, therefore, recommend placement

9. As a worker involved in locating absent parents, you have obtained information indicating that the address for the putative father is the same as the client's address.
   In order to determine whether, in fact, the client and putative father are living together, of the following, it would be MOST appropriate to
   A. visit the address and question the neighbors and superintendent about the putative father
   B. visit the client to ask her why she has concealed the fact that the putative father is living with her
   C. file the information in the case folder and wait for confirming information
   D. close the client's case and issue a recoupment notice to the putative father

10. A client claims that she never received a welfare check that was due her. As part of your investigation of her claim, you obtain from the bank a copy of the check, which has been endorsed with her name and cashed.
    Of the following, the BEST procedure for you to follow in this investigation is to
    A. end the investigation immediately, since the client's claim cannot be proved
    B. interview the client and show her the copy of the cashed check
    C. tell the client that you have evidence that her claim is false
    D. say nothing about the cashed check and try to trap the client in a false statement

11. As part of the investigation to locate an absent father, you make a field visit to interview one of the father's friends. Before beginning the interview, you identify yourself to the friend and show him your official identification.
    For you to do this is, generally,
    A. *good practice*, because the friend will have proof that you are authorized to make such confidential investigations
    B. *poor practice*, because the friend may not answer your questions when he knows why you are interviewing him

C. *good practice*, because your supervisor can confirm from the friend that you actually made the interview
D. *poor practice*, because the friend may warn the absent father that your agency is looking for him

12. As a field office worker you are investigating a citizen's complaint charging a mother of three children with child neglect. The mother tells you that her husband has become depressed after losing his job and is often abusive to her, and that this situation has made her feel anxious and has made it difficult for her to care for the children properly.
Which one of the following is the BEST way for you to respond to this situation?
   A. Tell the mother that she must do everything possible to help her husband find a job
   B. Arrange to meet the husband so you can explain to him the consequences of his behavior
   C. Investigate the complaint, report your findings, and refer the family for counseling or other appropriate services
   D. Suggest that the family obtain homemaker services so that the mother can go to work

13. You are interviewing a client in his home as part of your investigation of an anonymous complaint that he has been receiving Medicaid fraudulently. During the interview, the client frequently interrupts your questions to discuss the hardships of his life and the bitterness he feels about his medical condition.
Of the following, the BEST way for you to deal with these discussions is to
   A. cut them off abruptly, since the client is probably just trying to avoid answering your questions
   B. listen patiently, since these discussions may be helpful to the client and may give you information for your investigation
   C. remind the client that you are investigating a complaint against him and he must answer directly
   D. seek to gain the client's confidence by discussing any personal or medical problems which you yourself may have

14. While interviewing an absent father to determine his ability to pay child support, you realize that his answers to some of your questions contradict his answers to other questions.
Of the following, the BEST way for you to try to get accurate information from the father is to
   A. confront him with his contradictory answers and demand an explanation from him
   B. use your best judgment as to which of his answers are accurate and question him accordingly
   C. tell him that he has misunderstood your questions and that he must clarify his answers
   D. ask him the same questions in different words and follow up his answers with related questions

15. You are assigned to investigate a complaint of child neglect made against a minority mother by her non-minority neighbor. During an interview with you, the neighbor states that the mother allows her children to run around the streets half-dressed till late at night, and adds: *Of course, what can you expect from any of those people anyway?*
Your MOST appropriate action is to
   A. end the investigation, since the neighbor is clearly too prejudiced to be reliable
   B. tell the mother that the neighbor has made a complaint of child neglect against her
   C. seek evidence to support the complaint of child neglect made by the neighbor
   D. continue the interview with the neighbor in an attempt to get at the root of his prejudice against the mother

16. You are interviewing a couple with regard to available services for the husband's aged mother. During the interview, the husband casually mentions that he and his wife are thinking about becoming foster parents and would like to get some information on foster care programs offered through the Department of Social Services.
Of the following agencies within social services, the MOST appropriate one for you to refer this couple to is
   A. family and adult services
   B. special services for children
   C. bureau of child support
   D. special services for adults

17. You have been helping one of your clients to obtain medical assistance for her two young children. Accidentally, you obtain evidence that the client may be involved in a criminal scheme to collect duplicate welfare checks at several different addresses.
Of the following offices of the Department of Social Services, the MOST appropriate one to which you should report this evidence is
   A. the inspector general
   B. case intake and management
   C. the general counsel
   D. income support

Questions 18-25.

DIRECTIONS: Questions 18 through 25 are to be answered SOLELY on the basis of the Fact Situation and Report Form.

FACT SITUATION

On June 5, 2020, Mary Adams (Case No. 2095732), living at 1507 Montague Street, Apt. 3C, Brooklyn, New York, applied and was accepted for public assistance for herself and her three dependent children. Her husband, John, had left their home after an argument the previous week and had not returned, leaving Mrs. Adams without funds of any kind. She had tried to contact him at his place of employment, but was told that he had resigned several days prior to her call. When the case worker questioned Mrs. Adams about her husband's employment, income, and bank accounts, Mrs. Adams stated that he had done carpentry work during most of the years he had worked; his last known employer had been the Avco Lumber Company, 309 Amber Street, Queens, New York, where he had earned a weekly salary of $300. She then showed the case worker two bankbooks in her husband's name, which indicated a balance of $500 in one account and $275 in the other. A visit to Mr. Brown, a neighbor of the Adams', by the case worker, revealed that Mr. Adams had also told Mr. Brown about the existence of the bankbooks. A visit to the Avco Lumber Company by the case worker confirmed that Mr. Adams' gross salary had been $300 a week. This visit also revealed that Mr. Adams was a member of the Woodworkers' Union, Local #3, and that Mr. Adams' previous home address for the period February '09 to June '15 was 1109 Wellington Street, Brooklyn, New York.

REPORT FORM

A. **CLIENT**:
1. Name:_____
2. Address:_____
3. Case No:_____
4. Acceptance Date:_____
5. No. of Dependent Children:_____

B. **ABSENT PARENT**:
1. Name:_____
2. Date of Birth:_____
3. Place of Birth:_____
4. Present Address:_____
5. Regular Occupation:_____
6. Union Affiliation:_____
7. Name of Last Employer:_____
8. Address of Last Employer:_____
9. a. Weekly Earnings (Gross):_____
   b. How Verified:_____
10. a. Weekly Earnings (Net):_____
    b. How Verified:_____
11. a. Amount of Bank Accounts:_____
    b. How Verified:_____
12. Social Security No.:_____
13. Last Known Home Address:_____
14. Previous Address:_____

---

18. Based on the information given in the Fact Situation, the MOST appropriate of the following entries for Item B.11.b is:
    A. Revealed to case worker by Mrs. Adams
    B. Confirmed by visit to Mr. Brown
    C. Revealed by Woodworkers' Union, Local #7
    D. Confirmed by bankbooks shown by Mrs. Adams

18.____

7 (#1)

19. The one of the following which BEST answers Item B.4 is
    A. Unknown
    B. c/o Avco Lumber Company
    C. 1109 Wellington Street, Brooklyn, New York
    D. 1507 Montague Street, Brooklyn, New York

20. Based on the information given in the Fact Situation, it is NOT possible to answer Item
    A. A.2 B. A.5 C. B.6 D. B.10

21. The one of the following which would be LEAST helpful in tracing the missing parent is information found in Item
    A. B.12 B. B.10.a C. B.6 D. B.1

22. Based on the information given in the Fact Situation, it is MOST likely that the same entry would be made for Items
    A. A.1 and B.1
    B. A.4 and B.2
    C. B.9.a and B.10.a
    D. A.2 and B.13

23. Based on the information in the Fact Situation, the entry: 1109 Wellington Street, Brooklyn, New York would MOST likely be placed for Item
    A. A.2 B. B.4 C. B.8 D. B.14

24. The one of the following items that can be answered based on the information given in the Fact Situation is
    A. B.2 B. B.3 C. B.9.b D. B.12

25. Based on the information given in the Fact Situation, the figure 775 would appear in the entry for
    A. A.3 B. B.12 C. B.9.a D. B.11.a

KEY (CORRECT ANSWERS)

1. B
2. C
3. C
4. B
5. D

6. D
7. C
8. B
9. A
10. B

11. A
12. C
13. B
14. D
15. C

16. B
17. A
18. D
19. A
20. D

21. B
22. D
23. D
24. C
25. D

TEST 2

DIRECTIONS: Each question or incomplete statement is followed by several suggested answers or completions. Select the one that BEST answers the question or completes the statement. *PRINT THE LETTER OF THE CORRECT ANSWER IN THE SPACE AT THE RIGHT.*

1. A worker in a senior adult center is approached by one of his clients, an elderly man living alone and suffering from severe arthritis, who asks him how to go about obtaining homemaker services through the Department of Social Services.
   Of the following, the MOST appropriate office of the department to which the worker should refer this client is
   A. income support
   B. protective services for adults
   C. income maintenance
   D. case intake and management

   1.____

2. Workers assigned to locate absent parents frequently ask various governmental agencies to search their records for information useful in determining the address of the person they are seeking.
   Of the following, which is likely to be useful MOST frequently for this purpose is the
   A. motor vehicle bureau
   B. office of the district attorney
   C. department of investigation
   D. health and hospitals corporation

   2.____

Questions 3-7.

DIRECTIONS: Questions 3 through 7 are to be answered SOLELY on the basis of the following Fact Situation and Preliminary Investigation Form.

FACT SITUATION

COMPLAINT:
On March 1, Mrs. Mona Willard, a neighbor of the Smith family, reported to the Police Department that the Smith children were being severely neglected, and she requested that an investigation be conducted. She based her complaint on the fact that, since the time three weeks ago when Janet Smith's husband, Charles, deserted Mrs. Smith and their two children, John, age 2, and Darlene, age 4, the children have been seen wandering in the neighborhood at all hours, inadequately dressed against the cold.

INVESTIGATION:
Investigation by the Police Department and the Department of Social Services revealed that the above charge was true and, further, that Mrs. Smith had inflicted cruel and harsh physical treatment upon the children in an attempt to discipline them. The children were immediately removed from their parent's care and placed in a medical facility for tests and observation. It was found that the children were suffering from serious malnutrition and anemia and that they also showed signs of emotional disturbance.

2 (#2)

CASE ACTION DECISION:
Conferences which you, the case worker, have held with Dr. Charles Jordan, a physician treating Mrs. Smith, and with Ellen Farraday, a psychiatric social worker from the Mental Health Consultation Center, confirm that Mrs. Smith is emotionally unstable at the present time and cannot care for her children. A written report from the Chief Resident Physician at the hospital where the children have been placed indicates that both children are presently doing well, but when released will need the security of an emotionally stable atmosphere. It has therefore been decided that placement in a foster home is necessary for the children until such time as Mrs. Smith is judged to be capable of caring for them.

PRELIMINARY INVESTIGATION FORM

1. Child(ren) in Need of Protection:
   a. Name(s):_____
   b. Age(s):_____

2. Alleged Perpetrator:
   a. Name_____
   b. Relationship_____

3. Present Status of Child(ren):
   ☐ a. Remaining with Subject Pending Investigation
   ☐ b. Removed to Relatives
   ☐ c. Removed to Foster Care
   ☐ d. In Hospital
   ☐ e. Other

4. Actions or Services Needed for Child(ren)
   ☐ a. Housekeeper
   ☐ b. Homemaker
   ☐ c. Day Care
   ☐ d. Home Attendant
   ☐ e. Relatives
   ☐ f. Foster Care

5. Contacts Made to Support Case Action Decision

	I Phone	II Personal	III Written
a. Medical; School	☐	☐	☐
b. Relatives	☐	☐	☐
c. Social Agency	☐	☐	☐
d. Other	☐	☐	☐

3. The one of the following that should be entered in space 2.b is   3.____
    A. mother   B. father   C. neighbor   D. physician

4. The one of the following boxes that should be checked in Item 3 is   4.____
    A. a   B. c   C. d   D. e

5. The one of the following boxes that should be checked in Item 4 is   5.____
    A. a   B. c   C. d   D. f

6. Based on the information given in the Fact Situation, the boxes that should be   6.____
   checked off in Item 5 are:
   A. a-II, a-III, C-II   B. a-II, c-II, c-III
   C. a-I, a-II, a-III   D. b-II, c-I, c-II

7. The one of the following that would CORRECTLY appear as part of the entry

Questions 8-12.

DIRECTIONS: Questions 8 through 12 are to be answered SOLELY on the basis of the information contained in the following passage.

It is desirable, whenever possible, to have long-term elderly patients return to their own homes after hospitalization, provided that the medical condition is not acute. Of course, there must be room for the patient; the family must be able to provide some necessary care; and a physician's services must be available. Although the patient's family may be able to provide most services for the patient in his own home, this is generally unlikely because of the nature of the illness and the patient's need for a variety of services. Recently, hospital personnel, public health workers, visiting nurse associations, and community leaders have been developing home-care programs, which make the services of the hospital available to the patient who is not ill enough to require the concentrated technical facilities of a general hospital, but who is unable to attend an outpatient clinic or a physician's office. These services are those of the physician, visiting nurse, physical therapist, occupational therapist, social worker, and homemaker, as needed. There is also provision for readmission to the hospital for specific purposes and return to home care.

8. According to the above passage, it would be UNDESIRABLE to have an elderly   8.____
   patient return to his own home after hospitalization when the patient
   A. requires the services of doctor
   B. may be in immediate danger due to his medical condition
   C. is under physical or occupational therapy
   D. cannot go to the outpatient clinic of the hospital

9. According to the above passage, the *services of the hospital* which are made   9.____
   available by home-care programs include those of
   A. dietitians   B. visiting nurses
   C. public health administers   D. community workers

10. The one of the following statements about home-care programs which is BEST   10.____
    supported by the above paragraph is that home-care programs
    A. have been developed in part by hospital personnel
    B. relieve workloads of hospital personnel
    C. decrease public expenditures for hospitalization of the elderly
    D. reduce readmissions of elderly patients to hospitals

11. According to the above passage, home-care programs would be LEAST likely   11.____
    to include the services of a
    A. homemaker   B. social worker
    C. physician   D. hospital technician

12. It may be inferred from the above passage that a MAJOR purpose of home-care programs is to
    A. increase the demand for physicians, nurses, and other medical personnel
    B. provide patients in their homes with services similar to those provided in hospitals
    C. reduce the need for general hospitals and outpatient clinics
    D. relieve the family of their responsibility of caring for the patient

Questions 13-17.

DIRECTIONS: Questions 13 through 17 are to be answered SOLELY on the basis of the information contained in the following Duties Statement.

DUTIES STATEMENT OF THE VIOLATION CENTER (VC) CASE WORKER

1. Receives telephone, mail, and in-person reports of suspected violations from mandated and non-mandated sources, as well as from the New York State Violation Bureau (NYSVB), on form DSS-555, within 48 hours, to the Central Office of VC, 265 Church Street, New York, N.Y.

2. Completes in-office portion of DSS-555 received from mandated sources as fully as possible. Checks that report summary is specific, factual, and detailed. (See NYSVB instructions on Page 213)

3. When DSS-555 is received, clears Central Office of VC for any previous record of violation on file in Central Office. If record exists, enters additional information from file record on to DSS-555. Also requests Central Office Clerk to provide appropriate record number of previous record and enters additional information from file record on to DSS-555. Also requests Central Office Clerk to provide appropriate record number of previous record and enters it in correct box on form.

4. Determines appropriate Central Office Sex Code and Reporting Source Code for each violation. (The Codes are in the VC Manual.) The codes are then entered on the bottom of the reverse side of the DSS-555.

5. Determines appropriate Service Area Code for the address in the summary. The address is the location of the violation, if known. (If the location of the violation is unknown, the address of the primary witness shall be used.) Enters Service Area Code on reverse of DSS-555. All report summaries involving violations by N.Y.C. employees are sent to the Manhattan Borough Office of VC for clearance and transmittal to BEM.

---

13. According to the above Duties Statement, when a report of a suspected violation is received, a written summary of their report on DSS-555 must be sent within 48 hours by
    A. mandated sources
    B. non-mandated sources
    C. the NYSVB
    D. mandated and non-mandated sources, as well as by the NYSVB

14. From the above Duties Statement, it may be *inferred* that the case worker whose duties are described is MOST likely assigned to
    A. the Manhattan Borough Office of VC
    B. the New York State Violation Bureau
    C. the Central Office of VC
    D. BEM

    14.____

15. According to the above Duties Statement, the Central Office Sex Code is entered on the DSS-555
    A. on the opposite side from the Service Area Code
    B. on the front of the form
    C. above the Service Area Code on the form
    D. on the bottom of the back of the form

    15.____

16. According to the above Duties Statement, a case worker can determine the appropriate Reporting Source Code for a violation by consulting
    A. NYSVB Instructions
    B. the Central Office Clerk
    C. the VC Manual
    D. the Service Area Code

    16.____

17. As used in paragraph 2 of the above Duties Statement, the word *detailed* means MOST NEARLY
    A. full descriptive
    B. complicated
    C. of considerable length
    D. well-written

    17.____

Questions 18-25.

DIRECTIONS: Questions 18 through 25 are to be answered SOLELY on the basis of the following Semi-Monthly Family Allowance Schedule for Maintenance of Legally Responsible Relative (Figure No. 1) and Conversion Table (Figure 2) given on the following pages and the information and case situations given below).

FIGURE NO. 1

SEMI-MONTHLY FAMILY ALLOWANCE SCHEDULE FOR MAINTENANCE OF LEGALLY RESPONSIBLE RELATIVE AND DEPENDENTS BASED UPON TOTAL NUMBER OF PERSONS IN PRESENT HOUSEHOLD. (ALL SURPLUS IS TO BE USED AS CONTRIBUTION TO RECIPIENTS OF PUBLIC ASSISTANCE.)

TOTAL NUMBER OF PERSONS IN PRESENT HOUSEHOLD	ONE	TWO	THREE	FOUR	FIVE	SIX	EACH ADDITIONAL PERSON
SEMI-MONTHLY FAMILY ALLOWANCE	$1,600	$1,915	$2,200	$2,605	$2,800	$3,205	$350

FIGURE NO. 2
CONVERSION TABLE – WEEKLY TO SEMI-MONTHLY AMOUNTS

DOLLARS				CENTS			
Weekly Amount	Semi-Monthly Amount	Weekly Amount	Semi-Monthly Amount	Weekly Amount	Semi-Monthly Amount	Weekly Amount	Semi-Monthly Amount
$10	$21.70	$510.00	$1105.00	$0.10	$0.20	$5.10	$11.10
20.00	86.70	520.00	1126.70	0.20	0.40	5.20	11.30
30.00	65.00	530.00	1148.30	0.30	0.70	5.30	11.50
40.00	86.70	540.00	1170.00	0.40	0.90	5.40	11.70
50.00	108.30	550.00	1191.70	0.50	1.10	5.50	11.90
60.00	130.00	560.00	1213.30	0.60	1.30	5.60	12.10
70.00	151.70	570.00	1235.00	0.70	1.50	5.70	12.40
80.00	173.30	580.00	1256.70	1.00	1.70	5.80	12.60
90.00	195.00	590.00	1278.30	0.90	2.00	5.90	12.80
100.00	216.70	600.00	1300.00	1.00	2.20	6.00	13.00
110.00	238.30	610.00	1321.70	1.10	2.40	6.10	13.20
120.00	260.00	620.00	1343.30	1.20	2.60	6.20	13.40
130.00	281.70	630.00	1365.00	1.30	2.80	6.30	13.70
140.00	303.30	640.00	1386.70	1.40	3.00	6.40	13.90
150.00	325.00	650.00	1408.30	1.50	3.30	6.50	14.10
160.00	346.70	660.00	1430.00	1.60	3.50	6.60	14.30
170.00	368.30	670.00	1451.40	1.70	3.70	6.70	14.50
180.00	390.00	680.00	1473.30	1.80	3.90	6.80	14.70
190.00	411.70	690.00	1495.00	1.90	4.10	6.90	15.00
200.00	433.30	700.00	1516.70	2.00	4.30	7.00	15.20
210.00	455.00	710.00	1538.30	2.10	4.60	7.10	15.40
220.00	476.70	720.00	1560.00	2.20	4.80	7.20	15.60
230.00	498.30	730.00	1581.70	2.30	5.00	7.30	15.80
240.00	520.00	740.00	1603.30	2.40	5.20	7.40	16.00
250.00	541.70	750.00	1625.00	2.50	5.40	7.50	16.30
260.00	563.30	760.00	1646.70	2.60	5.60	7.60	16.50
270.00	585.00	770.00	1668.30	2.70	5.90	7.70	16.70
280.00	606.70	780.00	690.00	2.80	6.10	7.80	16.90
290.00	628.30	790.00	1711.70	2.90	6.30	7.90	17.10
300.00	650.00	800.00	1733.30	3.00	6.50	8.00	17.30
310.00	671.70	810.00	1755.00	3.10	6.70	8.10	17.60
320.00	693.30	820.00	1776.70	3.20	6.90	8.20	17.80
330.00	715.00	830.00	1798.30	3.30	7.20	8.30	18.00
340.00	736.70	840.00	1820.00	3.40	7.40	8.40	18.20
350.00	783.00	850.00	1841.70	3.50	7.60	8.50	18.40
360.00	780.00	860.00	1863.30	3.60	7.80	8.60	18.60
370.00	801.70	870.00	1885.00	3.70	8.00	8.70	18.90
380.00	823.30	880.00	1906.70	3.80	8.20	8.80	19.10
390.00	845.00	890.00	1928.30	3.90	8.50	8.90	19.30
400.00	866.70	900.00	1950.00	4.00	8.70	9.00	19.50
410.00	888.30	910.00	1971.70	4.10	8.90	9.10	19.70
420.00	910.00	920.00	1993.30	4.20	9.10	9.20	19.90
430.00	931.70	930.00	2015.00	4.30	9.30	9.30	20.20
440.00	953.30	940.00	2036.70	40.40	9.50	9.40	20.40
450.00	975.00	950.00	2058.30	40.50	9.80	9.50	20.60
460.00	996.70	960.00	2080.00	4.60	10.00	9.60	20.80
470.00	1018.30	970.00	2101.70	4.70	10.20	9.70	21.00
480.00	1040.00	980.00	2123.30	4.80	10.40	9.80	21.20
490.00	1061.70	990.00	2145.00	4.90	10.60	9.90	21.50
500.00	1083.30	1000.00	2166.70	5.00	10.80		

7 (#2)

INFORMATION

Legally responsible relatives living apart from persons on public assistance are asked to contribute toward the support of these persons. The amount of contribution depends on several factors, such as the number of persons in the legally responsible relative's present household who are dependent on his income (including himself), the amount of his gross income, and his expenses incident to employment. Since his contribution is computed on a semi-monthly basis, all figures must be broken down into semi-monthly amounts. Weekly amounts can be converted into semi-monthly amounts by using the conversion table on page 6.

The amount of supported is computed as follows:

1. Determine total weekly gross income (the wages or salary before payroll deductions) of legally responsible relative.
2. Deduct all weekly expenses incident to employment such as federal, state, and city income taxes, Social Security payments, State Disability Insurance payments, union dues, cost of transportation, and $10.00 maximum per work day for lunch.
3. Remaining income shall be considered as weekly net income of legally responsible relative.
4. Convert weekly net income to semi-monthly net income, using data in Figure No. 2.
5. Semi-monthly net income is compared to the semi-monthly allowance (see Figure No. 1). If there is an excess of net income, then that amount is considered available as the contribution to the public assistance household. If the semi-monthly allowance is greater than the semi-monthly net income, then there is an income deficit, and there is no income available as a contribution to the public assistance household.
6. The formula for computing the semi-monthly contribution is:
Semi-Monthly Net Income • Semi-Monthly Family Allowance = Semi-Monthly Amount of Income Available Towards Contribution to Public Assistance Household

Case Situation No. 1:

Mr. Andrew Young is separated from his wife and family and lives with one dependent in a 3-room furnished apartment. Mr. Young is employed as a dishwasher and his gross wages are $1,000 per week. He is employed 5 days a week and spends $14.40 a day for carfare. He spends $20.00 a work day on lunch. His weekly salary deductions are as follows:

Federal Income Tax	$142.30
State Income Tax	26.00
City Income Tax	9.80
Social Security	62.10
New York State Disability Insurance	5.30
Union Due	5.00

Mr. Young's wife and two children, for whom he is legally responsible, are currently receiving public assistance.

18. The weekly amount that Mr. Young contributes toward Social Security, New York State Disability Insurance, Income Taxes, and Union Dues is MOST NEARLY
    A. $214.70   B. $250.50   C. $320.50   D. $370.50

19. The total amount of all weekly expenses incident to Mr. Young's employment which should be deducted from his weekly gross earnings is MOST NEARLY
    A. $214.70   B. $250.50   C. $370.50   D. $420.50

20. Which one of the following amounts is Mr. Young's semi-monthly net income?
    A. $1259.00   B. $1363.90   C. $1623.90   D. $1701.50

21. The semi-monthly amount of income available to the contribution to Mr. Young's wife and two children is MOST NEARLY
    A. $0.00   B. $23.90   C. $236.10   D. $551.10

Case Situation No. 2:

Mr. Donald Wilson resides with six dependents in a seven-room unfurnished apartment. Mr. Wilson is employed as an automobile salesman and his gross wages are $4,000 per week. He is employed five days a week and spends $10.00 a day carfare. He spends $50.00 a work day for lunch. His weekly salary deductions are as follows:

Federal Income Tax	$$705.50
State Income Tax	150.00
City Income Tax	97.00
Social Security	301.00
New York State Disability Insurance	52.50
Union Due	Not Union Member

22. The weekly amount that Mr. Wilson contributes toward Social Security, New York State Disability Insurance, Federal Income Tax, and Union Dues is MOST NEARLY
    A. $1059.00   B. $1159.00   C. $1306.00   D. $1406.00

23. The total amount of all weekly expenses incident to Mr. Wilson's employment, which should be deducted from his weekly gross earnings is MOST NEARLY
    A. $1159.00   B. $1306.00   C. $1406.00   D. $1606.00

24. The semi-monthly family allowance for Mr. Wilson and his six dependents is MOST NEARLY
    A. $2594.00   B. $3205.00   C. $1406.00   D. $4000.00

25. The semi-monthly amount Mr. Wilson's income available for contribution to his wife and child is MOST NEARLY
    A. $1633.00   B. $2065.40   C. $2594.00   D. $2810.20

KEY (CORRECT ANSWERS)

1. D
2. A
3. A
4. C
5. D

6. A
7. C
8. B
9. B
10. A

11. D
12. B
13. A
14. C
15. D

16. C
17. A
18. B
19. C
20. B

21. A
22. A
23. C
24. C
25. B

EXAMINATION SECTION
TEST 1

DIRECTIONS: Each question or incomplete statement is followed by several suggested answers or completions. Select the one that BEST answers the question or completes the statement. *PRINT THE LETTER OF THE CORRECT ANSWER IN THE SPACE AT THE RIGHT.*

1. An interview is BEST conducted in private primarily because 1.____
   A. the person interviewed will tend to be less self-conscious
   B. the interviewer will be able to maintain his continuity of thought better
   C. it will insure that the interview is "off the record"
   D. people tend to "show off" before an audience

2. An interviewer can BEST establish a good relationship with the person being interviewed by 2.____
   A. assuming casual interest in the statements made by the person being interviewed
   B. taking the point of view of the person interviewed
   C. controlling the interview to a major extent
   D. showing a genuine interest in the person

3. An interviewer will be better able to understand the person interviewed and his problems if he recognizes that much of the person's behavior is due to motives 3.____
   A. which are deliberate   B. of which he is unaware
   C. which are inexplicable   D. which are kept under control

4. An interviewer's attention must be directed toward himself as well as toward the person interviewed. 4.____
   This statement means that the interviewer should
   A. keep in mind the extent to which his own prejudices may influence his judgment
   B. rationalize the statements made by the person interviewed
   C. gain the respect and confidence of the person interviewed
   D. avoid being too impersonal

5. More complete expression will be obtained from a person being interviewed if the interviewer can create the impression that 5.____
   A. the data secured will become part of a permanent record
   B. official information must be accurate in every detail
   C. it is the duty of the person interviewed to give accurate data
   D. the person interviewed is participating in a discussion of his own problems

6. The practice of asking leading questions should be avoided in an interview because the
   A. interviewer risks revealing his attitudes to the person being interviewed
   B. interviewer may be led to ignore the objective attitudes of the person interviewed
   C. answers may be unwarrantedly influenced
   D. person interviewed will resent the attempt to lead him and will be less cooperative

7. A good technique for the interviewer to use in an effort to secure reliable data and to reduce the possibility of misunderstanding is to
   A. use casual undirected conversation, enabling the person being interviewed to talk about himself, and thus secure the desired information
   B. adopt the procedure of using direct questions regularly
   C. extract the desired information from the person being interviewed by putting him on the defensive
   D. explain to the person being interviewed the information desired and the reason for needing it

8. You are interviewing a patient to determine whether she is eligible for medical assistance. Of the many questions that you have to ask her, some are routine questions that patients tend to answer willingly and easily. Other questions are more personal and some patients tend to resent being asked them and avoid answering them directly.
   For you to begin the interview with the more personal questions would be
   A. *desirable*, because the end of the interview will go smoothly and the patient will be left with a warm feeling
   B. *undesirable*, because the patient might not know the answers to the questions
   C. *desirable*, because you will be able to return to these questions later to verify the accuracy of the responses
   D. *undesirable*, because you might antagonize the patient before you have had a chance to establish rapport

9. While interviewing a patient about her family composition, the patient asks you whether you are married.
   Of the following, the MOST appropriate way for you to handle this situation is to
   A. answer the question briefly and redirect her back to the topic under discussion
   B. refrain from answering the question and proceed with the interview
   C. advise the patient that it is more important that she answer your questions than that you answer hers, and proceed with the interview
   D. promise the patient that you will answer her question later, in the hope that she will forget, and redirect her back to the topic under discussion

10. In response to a question about his employment history, a patient you are interviewing rambles and talks about unrelated matters.
    Of the following, the MOST appropriate course of action for you to take FIRST is to

A. ask questions to direct the patient back to his employment history
B. advise him to concentrate on your questions and not to discuss irrelevant information
C. ask him why he is resisting a discussion of his employment history
D. advise him that if you cannot get the information you need, he will not be eligible for medical assistance

11. Suppose that a person you are interviewing becomes angry at some of the questions you have asked, calls you meddlesome and nosy, and states that she will not answer those questions.
Of the following, which is the BEST action for you to take?
    A. Explain the reasons the questions are asked and the importance of the answers
    B. Inform the interviewee that you are only doing your job and advise her that she should answer your questions or leave the office
    C. Report to your supervisor what the interviewee called you and refuse to continue the interview
    D. End the interview and tell the interviewee she will not be serviced by your department

11.____

12. Suppose that during the course of an interview the interviewee demands in a very rude way that she be permitted to talk to your supervisor or someone in charge.
Which of the following is probably the BEST way to handle this situation?
    A. Inform your supervisor of the demand and ask her to speak to the interviewee
    B. Pay no attention to the demands of the interviewee and continue the interview
    C. Report to your supervisor and tell her to get another interviewer for this interviewee
    D. Tell her you are the one "in charge" and that she should talk to you

12.____

13. Of the following, the outcome of an interview by an aide depends MOST heavily on the
    A. personality of the interviewee
    B. personality of the aide
    C. subject matter of the questions asked
    D. interaction between aide and interviewee

13.____

14. Some patients being interviewed are primarily interested in making a favorable impression.
The aide should be aware of the fact that such patients are more likely than other patients to
    A. try to anticipate the answers the interviewer is looking for
    B. answer all questions openly and frankly
    C. try to assume the role of interviewer
    D. be anxious to get the interview over as quickly as possible

14.____

15. The type of interview which an aide usually conducts is substantially different from most interviewing situations in all of the following aspects EXCEPT the
    A. setting
    B. kinds of clients
    C. techniques employed
    D. kinds of problems

16. During an interview, an aide uses a "leading question."
    This type of question is so-called because it generally
    A. starts a series of questions about one topic
    B. suggests the answer which the aide wants
    C. forms the basis for a following "trick" question
    D. sets, at the beginning, the tone of the interview

17. Casework interviewing is always directed to the client and his situation.
    The one of the following which is the MOST accurate statement with respect to the proper focus of an interview is that the
    A. caseworker limits the client to concentration on objective data
    B. client is generally permitted to talk about facts and feelings with no direction from the caseworker
    C. main focus in casework interviews is on feelings rather than facts
    D. caseworker is responsible for helping the client focus on any material which seems to be related to his problems or difficulties

18. Assume that you are conducting a training program for the caseworkers under your supervision. At one of the sessions, you discuss the problem of interviewing a dull and stupid client who gives a slow and disconnected case history.
    The BEST of the following interviewing methods for you to recommend in such a case in order to ascertain facts is for the caseworker to
    A. ask the client leading questions requiring "yes" or "no" answers
    B. request the client to limit his narration to the essential facts so that the interview can be kept as brief as possible
    C. review the story with the client, patiently asking simple questions
    D. tell the client that unless he is more cooperative he cannot be helped to solve his problem

19. A recent development in casework interviewing procedure, known as multiple-client interviewing, consists of interviews of the entire family at the same time. However, this may not be an effective casework method in certain situations.
    Of the following, the situation in which the standard individual interview would be preferable is when
    A. family member derive consistent and major gratification from assisting each other in their destructive responses
    B. there is a crucial family conflict to which the members are reacting
    C. the family is overwhelmed by interpersonal anxieties which have not been explored
    D. the worker wants to determine the pattern of family interaction to further his diagnostic understanding

20. A follow-up interview was arranged for an applicant in order that he could furnish 20._____
certain requested evidence. At this follow-up interview, the applicant still fails
to furnish the necessary evidence.
It would be MOST advisable for you to
   A. advise the applicant that he is now considered ineligible
   B. ask the applicant how soon he can get the necessary evidence and set a
      date for another interview
   C. question the applicant carefully and thoroughly to determine if he has
      misrepresented or falsified any information
   D. set a date for another interview and tell the applicant to get the necessary
      evidence by that time

KEY (CORRECT ANSWERS)

1.	A	11.	A
2.	D	12.	A
3.	B	13.	D
4.	A	14.	A
5.	D	15.	C
6.	C	16.	B
7.	D	17.	D
8.	D	18.	C
9.	A	19.	A
10.	A	20.	B

TEST 2

DIRECTIONS: Each question or incomplete statement is followed by several suggested answers or completions. Select the one that BEST answers the question or completes the statement. *PRINT THE LETTER OF THE CORRECT ANSWER IN THE SPACE AT THE RIGHT.*

1. In interviewing, the practice of anticipating an applicant's answers to questions is generally
    A. *desirable*, because it is effective and economical when it is necessary to interview large numbers of applicants
    B. *desirable*, because many applicants have language difficulties
    C. *undesirable*, because it is the inalienable right of every person to answer as he sees fit
    D. *undesirable*, because applicants may tend to agree with the answer proposed by the interviewer even when the answer is not entirely correct

2. When an initial interview is being conducted, one way of starting is to explain the purpose of the interview to the applicant.
    The practice of starting the interview with such an explanation is generally
    A. *desirable*, because the applicant can then understand why the interview is necessary and what will be accomplished by it
    B. *desirable*, because it creates the rapport which is necessary to successful interviewing
    C. *undesirable*, because time will be saved by starting directly with the questions which must be asked
    D. *undesirable*, because the interviewer should have the choice of starting an interview in any manner he prefers

3. For you to use responses such as "That's interesting," "Uh-huh," and "Good" during an interview with a patient is
    A. *desirable*, because they indicate that the investigator is attentive
    B. *undesirable*, because they are meaningless to the patient
    C. *desirable*, because the investigator is not supposed to talk excessively
    D. *undesirable*, because they tend to encourage the patient to speak freely

4. During the course of a routine interview, the BEST tone of voice for an interviewer to use is
    A. authoritative   B. uncertain
    C. formal   D. conversational

5. It is recommended that interviews which inquire into the personal background of an individual should be held in private.
    The BEST reason for this practice is that privacy
    A. allows the individual to talk freely about the details of his background
    B. induces contemplative thought on the part of the interviewed individual
    C. prevents any interruptions by departmental personnel during the interview
    D. most closely resembles the atmosphere of the individual's personal life

6. Assume that you are interviewing a patient to determine whether he has any savings accounts.
   To obtain this information, the MOST effective way to phrase your question would be:
   A. "You don't have any savings, do you?"
   B. "At which bank do you have a savings account?"
   C. "Do you have a savings account?"
   D. "May I assume that you have a savings account?"

7. You are interviewing a patient who is not cooperating to the extent necessary to get all required information. Therefore, you decide to be more forceful in your approach.
   In this situation, such a course of action is
   A. *advisable*, because such a change in approach may help to increase the patient's participation
   B. *advisable*, because you will be using your authority more effectively
   C. *inadvisable*, because you will not be able to change this approach if it doesn't produce results
   D. *inadvisable*, because an aggressive approach generally reduces the validity of the interview

8. You have attempted to interview a patient on two separate occasions, and both attempts were unsuccessful. The patient has been totally uncooperative and you sense a personal hostility toward you.
   Of the following, the BEST way to handle this type of situation would be to
   A. speak to the patient in a courteous manner and ask him to explain exactly what he dislikes about you
   B. inform the patient that you will not allow personality conflicts to disrupt the interview
   C. make no further attempt to interview the patient and recommend that he be billed in full
   D. discuss the problem with your supervisor and suggest that another investigator be assigned to try to interview the patient

9. At the beginning of an interview, a patient with normal vision tells you that he is reluctant to discuss his finances. You realize that it will be necessary in this case to ask detailed questions about his net income.
   When you begin this line of questioning, of the following, the LEAST important aspect you should consider is your
   A. precise wording of the question   B. manner of questioning
   C. tone of voice   D. facial expressions

10. A caseworker under your supervision has been assigned the task of interviewing a man who is applying for foster home placement for his two children. The caseworker seeks your advice as to how to question this man, stating that she finds the applicant to be a timid and self-conscious person who seems torn between the necessity of having to answer the worker's questions truthfully and the effect he thinks his answers will have on his application.

Of the following, the BEST method for the caseworker to use in order to determine the essential facts in this case is to
- A. assure the applicant that he need not worry since the majority of applications for foster home placement are approved
- B. delay the applicant's narration of the facts important to the case until his embarrassment and fears have been overcome
- C. ignore the statements made by the applicant and obtain all the required information from his friends and relatives
- D. inform the applicant that all statements made by him will be verified and are subject to the law governing perjury

11. Assume that a worker is interviewing a boy in his assigned group in order to help him find a job.
At the BEGINNING of the interview, the worker should
    - A. suggest a possible job for the youth
    - B. refer the youth to an employment agency
    - C. discuss the youth's work history and skills with him
    - D. refer the youth to the manpower and career development agency

11._____

12. As part of the investigation to locate an absent father, you make a field visit to interview one of the father's friends. Before beginning the interview, you identify yourself to the friend and show him your official identification.
For you to do this is, generally,
    - A. *good practice*, because the friend will have proof that you are authorized to make such confidential investigations
    - B. *poor practice*, because the friend may not answer your questions when he knows why you are interviewing him
    - C. *good practice*, because your supervisor can confirm from the friend that you actually made the interview
    - D. *poor practice*, because the friend may warn the absent father that your agency is looking for him

12._____

13. You are interviewing a client in his home as part of your investigation of an anonymous complaint that he has been receiving Medicaid fraudulently. During the interview, the client frequently interrupts your questions to discuss the hardships of his life and the bitterness he feels about his medical condition.
Of the following, the BEST way for you to deal with these discussions is to
    - A. cut them off abruptly, since the client is probably just trying to avoid answering your questions
    - B. listen patiently, since these discussions may be helpful to the client and may give you information for your investigation
    - C. remind the client that you are investigating a complaint against him and he must answer directly
    - D. seek to gain the client's confidence by discussing any personal or medical problems which you yourself may have

13._____

14. While interviewing an absent father to determine his ability to pay child support, you realize that his answers to some of your questions contradict his answers to other questions.
    Of the following, the BEST way for you to try to get accurate information from the father is to
    A. confront him with his contradictory answers and demand an explanation from him
    B. use your best judgment as to which of his answers are accurate and question him accordingly
    C. tell him that he has misunderstood your questions and that he must clarify his answers
    D. ask him the same questions in different words and follow up his answer with related questions

15. Assume that an applicant, obviously under a great deal of stress, talks continuously and rambles, making it difficult for you to determine the exact problem and her need.
    In order to make the interview more successful, it would be BEST for you to
    A. interrupt the applicant and ask her specific questions in order to get the information you need
    B. tell the applicant that her rambling may be a basic cause of her problem
    C. let the applicant continue talking as long as she wishes
    D. ask the applicant to get to the point because other people are waiting for you

16. A worker must be able to interview clients all day and still be able to listen and maintain interest.
    Of the following, it is MOST important for you to show interest in the client because, if you appear interested,
    A. the client is more likely to appreciate your professional status
    B. the client is more likely to disclose a greater amount of information
    C. the client is less likely to tell lie
    D. you are more likely to gain your supervisor's approval

17. When you are interviewing clients, it is important to notice and record how they say what they say—angrily, nervously, or with "body English"—because these signs may
    A. tell you that the client's words are the opposite of what the client feels and you may need to dig to find out what those feeling are
    B. be the prelude to violent behavior which no aide is prepared to handle
    C. show that the client does not really deserve serious consideration
    D. be important later should you be asked to defend what you did for the client

18. The patient you are interviewing is reticent and guarded in responding to your questions. He is not providing the information needed to complete his application for medical assistance.
    In this situation, the one of the following which is the MOST appropriate course of action for you to take FIRST is to

A. end the interview and ask him to contact you when he is ready to answer your questions
B. advise the patient that you cannot end the interview until he has provided all the information you need to complete the application
C. emphasize to the patient the importance of the questions and the need to answer them in order to complete the application
D. advise the patient that if he answers your questions the interview will be easier for both of you

19. At the end of an interview with a patient, he describes a problem he is having with his teenage son, who is often truant and may be using narcotics. The patient asks you for advice in handling his son.
Of the following, the MOST appropriate action for you to take is to
    A. make an appointment to see the patient and his son together
    B. give the patient a list of drug counseling programs to which he may refer his son
    C. suggest to the patient that his immediate concern should be his own hospitalization rather than his son's problem
    D. tell the patient that you are not qualified to assist him but will attempt to find out who can

19.____

20. A MOST appropriate condition in the use of direct questions to obtain personal data in an interview is that, whenever possible,
    A. the direct questions be used only as a means of encouraging the person interviewed to talk about himself
    B. provision be made for recording the information
    C. the direct questions be used only after all other methods have failed
    D. the person being interviewed understands the reason for requesting the information

20.____

KEY (CORRECT ANSWERS)

1.	D	11.	C
2.	A	12.	A
3.	A	13.	B
4.	D	14.	D
5.	A	15.	A
6.	B	16.	B
7.	A	17.	A
8.	D	18.	C
9.	A	19.	D
10.	B	20.	D

READING COMPREHENSION
UNDERSTANDING AND INTERPRETING WRITTEN MATERIAL

EXAMINATION SECTION

TEST 1

DIRECTIONS: Each question or incomplete statement is followed by several suggested answers or completions. Select the one that BEST answers the question or completes the statement. *PRINT THE LETTER OF THE CORRECT ANSWER IN THE SPACE AT THE RIGHT.*

Questions 1-4.

DIRECTIONS: Questions 1 through 4 are to be answered SOLELY on the basis of the information in the following paragraphs.

Some authorities have questioned whether the term *culture of poverty* should be used since *culture* means a design for living which is passed down from generation to generation. The culture of poverty is, however, a very useful concept if it is used with care, with recognition that poverty is a subculture, and with avoidance of the *cookie-cutter* approached. With regard to the individual, the cookie-cutter view assumes that all individuals in a culture turn out exactly alike, as if they were so many cookies. It overlooks the fact that, at least in our urban society, every individual is a member of more than one subculture; and which subculture most strongly influences his response in a given situation depends on the interaction of a great many factors, including his individual make-up and history, the specifics of the various subcultures to which he belongs, and the specifics of the given situation. It is always important to avoid the cookie-cutter view of culture, with regard to the individual and to the culture or subculture involved.

With regard to the culture as a whole, the cookie-cutter concept again assumes homogeneity and consistency. It forgets that within any one culture or subculture there are conflicts and contradictions, and that at any given moment an individual may have to choose, consciously, between conflicting values or patterns. Also, most individuals, in varying degrees, have a dual set of values—those by which they live and those they cherish as best. This point has been made and documented repeatedly about the culture of poverty.

1. The *cookie-cutter* approach assumes that   1.____
   A. members of the same *culture* are all alike
   B. *culture* stays the same from generation to generation
   C. the term *culture* should not be applied to groups who are poor
   D. there are value conflicts within most *cultures*

2. According to the above passage, every person in our cities   2.____
   A. is involved in the conflicts of urban culture
   B. recognizes that poverty is a subculture
   C. lives by those values too which he is exposed
   D. belongs to more than one subculture

3. The above passage emphasizes that a culture is likely to contain within it   3._____
   A. one dominant set of values
   B. a number of contradictions
   C. one subculture to which everyone belongs
   D. members who are exactly alike

4. According to the above passage, individuals are sometimes forced to choose BETWEEN   4._____
   A. cultures
   B. subcultures
   C. different sets of values
   D. a new culture and an old culture

Questions 5-8.

DIRECTIONS: Questions 5 through 8 are to be answered SOLELY on the basis of the following passage.

There are approximately 33 million poor people in the United States; 14.3 million of them are children, 5.3 million are old people, and the remainder are in other categories. Altogether, 6.5 million families live in poverty because the head of household cannot work; they are either too old or too sick or too severely handicapped, or they are widowed or deserted mothers of young children. There are the working poor: the low-paid workers, the workers in seasonal industries, and soldiers with no additional income who are heads of families. There are the underemployed: those who would like full-time jobs but cannot find them, those employees who would like year-round work but lack of opportunity, and those who are employed below their level of training. There are the non-working poor: the older men and women with small retirement incomes and those with no income, the disabled, the physically and mentally handicapped, and the chronically sick.

5. According to the above passage, approximately what percent of the poor people in the United States are children?   5._____
   A. 33   B. 16   C. 20   D. 44

6. According to the above passage, people who work in seasonal industries are LIKELY to be classified as   6._____
   A. working poor
   B. underemployed
   C. non-working poor
   D. low-paid workers

7. According to the above passage, the category of non-working poor includes people who   7._____
   A. receive unemployment insurance
   B. cannot find full-time work
   C. are disabled or mentally handicapped
   D. are soldiers with wives and children

8. According to the above passage, among the underemployed are those who   8._____
   A. can find only part-time work
   B. are looking for their first jobs
   C. are inadequately trained
   D. depend on insufficient retirement incomes

Questions 9-13.

DIRECTIONS: Read the Inter-office Memo below. Then, answer Questions 9 through 13 SOLELY on the basis of the memo.

INTER-OFFICE MEMORANDUM

To: Alma Robinson, Human Resources Aide

From: Frank Shields, Social Worker

I would like to have you help Mr. Edward Tunney, who is trying to raise his two children by himself. He needs to learn to improve the physical care of his children and especially of his daughter Helen, age 9. She is avoided and ridiculed at school because her hair is uncombed, her teeth not properly cleaned, her clothing torn, wrinkled and dirty, as well as shabby and poorly fitted. The teachers and school officials have contacted the Department and the social worker for two years about Helen. She is not able to make friends because of these problems. I have talked to Mr. Tunney about improvements for the child's clothing, hair, and hygiene. He tends to deny these things are problems, but is cooperative, and a second person showing him the importance of better physical care for Helen would be helpful.

Perhaps you could teach Helen how to fix her own hair. She has all the materials. I would also like you to form your own opinion of the sanitary conditions in the home and how they could be improved.

Mr. Tunney is expecting your visit and is willing to talk with you about ways he can help with these problems.

9. In the above memorandum, the Human Resources Aide is being asked to help Mr. Tunney to
    A. improve the learning habits of his children
    B. enable his children to make friends at school
    C. take responsibility for the upbringing of his children
    D. give attention to the grooming and cleanliness of his children

9.____

10. This case was brought to the attention of the social worker by
    A. government officials
    B. teachers and school officials
    C. the Department
    D. Mr. Tunney

10.____

11. In general, Mr. Tunney's attitude with regard to his children could BEST be described as
    A. interested in correcting the obvious problem, but unable to do so alone
    B. unwilling to follow the advice of those who are trying to help
    C. concerned but unaware of the seriousness of these problems
    D. interested in helping them, but afraid of taking the advice of the social worker

11.____

12. Which of the following actions has NOT been suggested as a possible step for 12.____
    the Human Resource Aide to take?
    A. Help Helen to learn to care for herself by teaching her grooming skills
    B Determine was of improvement gathered on a home visit
    C. Discuss her own views on Helen's problems with school officials
    D. Ask Mr. Tunney in what ways he believes the physical care may be
       improved

13. According to the above memo, the Human Resources Aide is ESPECIALLY 13.____
    being asked to observe and form her own opinions about
    A. the relationship between Mr. Tunney and the school officials
    B. Helen's attitude toward her classmates and teacher
    C. the sanitary conditions in the home
    D. the reasons Mr. Tunney is not cooperative with the agency

Questions 14-16.

DIRECTIONS: Questions 14 through 16 are to be answered SOLELY on the basis of the
              following paragraph.

   In social work, professional responsibility and accountability extend to a larger segment of
the general community than is true of the older professions which have more limited and more
specialized areas of community responsibility and public trust. Advances in knowledge about
both the nature of human institutions and the nature of the individual have placed social work in
the center of a vast complex of interrelationships. The situations that come to the attention of
the social worker, whatever his functions, may be the circumstances of an individual client or of
a group or of a community which may or may not be socially sanctioned, and the proposed
remedy may be considered desirable or questionable. When there is agreement between the
client group and the community on the nature of the problem and on the validity of the proposed
remedy, such agreement may lead to the establishment of social institutions. Complication
arise when the client or client group, or the community, does not accept the need for change or
is not in agreement with the social worker about the direction it should take. The social worker
has the obligation to pursue his objective regardless of the difficulties. Even if social work, as it
is practiced today, were to achieve the degree of acceptance afforded the older professions, it
would still find itself, with every new development, holding unorthodox and not very respectful
views on many aspects of personal and social relationships.

14. The MOST accurate of the following statements about the relationship 14.____
    between social work and the other professions is:
    A. Advances in knowledge have placed social work in a central position
       among the professions
    B. Although younger, social work has become basic to the older professions
       in their responsibility and accountability in the community
    C. It is the responsibility of social workers to hold unorthodox views on social
       relationships
    D. The areas of responsibility of social work within the community are more
       extensive than those of the older professions

15. When, because of an existing problem, a social worker has advocated a change in a social institution which has been opposed by the community, the social worker should
    A. attempt to surmount the opposition, continuing to seek to reach his objective
    B. change his position to gain the support of the community
    C. review the position that he has taken to see whether he cannot revise his objective to the point where it may gain community support
    D. work to achieve for his profession the degree of acceptance which is afforded the older professions

15._____

16. Of the following, the BEST title for the above paragraph is
    A. DANGERS OF SOCIAL RESPONSIBILITY
    B. SOCIAL WORK AND THE OLDER PROFESSION COMPARED
    C. SOCIAL WORKERS' RESPONSIBILITY IN SOCIAL CHANGE
    D. UNORTHODOX SOCIAL WORK

16._____

Questions 17-19.

DIRECTIONS: Questions 17 through 19 are to be answered SOLELY on the basis of the following paragraphs.

Toward the end of the 19th century, as social work principles and theories took form, areas of conflict between the responsibility of the social worker to the client group and to the status quo of social and economic institutions became highlighted. The lay public's attitude toward the individual poor was one of emphasis on betterment through the development of the individual's capacity for self-maintenance. They hoped to maintain this end both by helping the client to rely on his unused capacities for self-help and by facilitating is access to what were assumed to be the natural sources of help family, relatives, churches, and other charitable associations. Professional social workers were fast becoming aware of the need for social reform. They perceived that traditional methods of help were largely inadequate to cope with the factors that were creating poverty and maladjustment for a large number of the population faster than the charity societies could relieve such problems through individual effort. The critical view, held by social workers, of the character of many social institutions was not shared by other groups in the community who had not reached the same point of awareness about the deficiencies in the functioning of these institutions. Thus, the views of the social worker were beginning to differ, sometimes radically, from the basic views of large sections of the population.

17. The social workers of the late 19th century found themselves in conflict with the status quo CHIEFLY because they
    A. had become professionalized through the development of a body of theory and principles
    B. became aware that many social ills could not be cured through existing institutions
    C. felt that traditional methods of helping the poor must be expanded regardless of the cost to the public
    D. believed that the right of the individual to be self-determining should be emphasized

17._____

18. It was becoming apparent, by the end of the 19th century, that in relation to the needs of the poor, existing social institutions
    A. did not sufficiently emphasize the ability of the poor to utilize their natural sources of help
    B. were using the proper methods of helping the poor, but were hindered by the work of social workers who had broken with tradition
    C. were no longer capable of meeting the needs of the poor because the causes of poverty had changed
    D. were capable of meeting the needs of the poor, but needed more financial aid from the general public since the number of people in need had increased

18._____

19. Social workers at the end of the 19th century may be PROPERLY classified as
    A. growing in awareness that many social ills could be alleviated through social reform
    B. very perceptive individuals who realized that traditional methods of help were humiliating to the poor
    C. strong advocates of expanding the existing traditional sources of relief
    D. too radical because they favored easing life for the poor at the expense of increased taxation to the public at large

19._____

Questions 20-24.

DIRECTIONS: Questions 20 through 24 are to be answered SOLELY on the basis of the following paragraphs.

With the generation gap yawning before us, it is well to remember that 20 years ago teenagers produced a larger proportion of unwedlock births than today, and that the illegitimacy rate among teenagers is lower than among women in their twenties and thirties. In addition, the illegitimacy rate has risen less among teenagers than among older women.

It is helpful to note the difference between illegitimacy rate and illegitimacy ratio. The ratio is the number of illegitimate babies per 1,000 live births. The rate is the number of illegitimate births per 1,000 unmarried women of childbearing age. The ratio talks about babies; the rate talks about mothers. The ratio is useful for planning services, but worse than useless for considering trends since it depends on the age and marital composition of the population, illegitimacy rate, and the fertility of married women. For example, the ratio among girls under 18 is bound to be high in comparison with older women since few are married mothers. However, the illegitimacy rate is relatively low.

20. Of the following, the MOST suitable title for the above passage would be
    A. THE GENERATION GAP
    B. MORAL STANDARDS AND TEENAGE ILLEGITIMACY RATIO
    C. A COMPARISON OF ILLEGITIMACY RATE AND ILLEGITIMACY RATIO
    D. CAUSES OF HIGH ILLEGITIMACY RATES

20._____

21. According to the above passage, which of the following statements is CORRECT?
The illegitimacy
    A. rate has fallen among women in their thirties
    B. ratio is the number of illegitimate births per 1,000 unmarried women of childbearing age
    C. ratio is partially dependent on the illegitimacy rate
    D. rate is more useful than the ratio for planning services

22. According to the above passage, of the following age groups, the illegitimacy ratio would be expected to be HIGHEST in comparison with the other groups for the group aged
    A. 17   B. 21   C. 25   D. 29

23. According to the above passage, of the following age groups, the illegitimacy rate would be expected to be LOWEST in comparison with the other groups for the group aged
    A. 17   B. 21   C. 25   D. 29

24. As used in the above passage, the underlined word *composition* means MOST NEARLY
    A. essay   B. makeup   C. security   D. happiness

25. A document was published by a public agency and distributed for discussion. The document contained data showing trends in the level of reading among freshmen college students and suggested that the high schools were not investing enough effort in overcoming retardation. It compared the costs of intensifying reading instruction in the secondary schools as compared to costs in colleges for such instruction.
According to the above statement, it is REASONABLE to conclude that
    A. the document proposed new programs
    B. the college students read better than high school students
    C. some college students need remedial reading
    D. the study was done by a consultant

KEY (CORRECT ANSWERS)

1.	A	11.	C
2.	D	12.	C
3.	B	13.	C
4.	C	14.	D
5.	D	15.	A
6.	A	16.	C
7.	C	17.	B
8.	A	18.	C
9.	D	19.	A
10.	B	20.	C

21. C
22. A
23. A
24. B
25. C

TEST 2

DIRECTIONS: Each question or incomplete statement is followed by several suggested answers or completions. Select the one that BEST answers the question or completes the statement. *PRINT THE LETTER OF THE CORRECT ANSWER IN THE SPACE AT THE RIGHT.*

Questions 1-4.

DIRECTIONS: Questions 1 through 4 are to be answered SOLELY on the basis of the following paragraph.

    Form W-280 provides a uniform standard for estimating family expenses and is used as a basis for determining eligibility for the care of children at public expense. The extent to which legally responsible relatives can pay for the care of a child must be computed. The minimum amount of the payment required from legally responsible relatives shall be 50% of the budget surplus as computed on Form W-281, plus any governmental benefits, such as OASDI benefits, or Railroad Retirement benefits being paid to a family member for the child receiving care or services. Because of the kinds and quantities of services included in the budget schedule (W-280) and because only 50% of the budget surplus is required as payment, no allowances for special needs are made, except for verified payments into civil service pension funds, amounts paid to a garnishee, or amounts paid to another agency for the care of other relatives for whom the relative is legally responsible, or for other such expenses if approval has been granted after Form W-278 has been submitted. In determining the income of the legally responsible relative, income from wages, self-employment, unemployment insurance benefits, and any such portion of governmental benefits as is not specifically designated for children already receiving care is to be included. Should 50% of the family's surplus meet the child care expenses, the case shall not be processed. Form W-279, an agreement to support, shall be signed by the legally responsible relative when 50% of the surplus is $1.00 or more a week.

1. A family is required to sign an agreement to support
   A. whenever they are legally responsible for the support of the child under care
   B. before any care at public expense is given to the child
   C. when their income surplus is at least $2.00/week
   D. when 50% of their income surplus meets the full needs of the child

2. The reason for allowing a family to deduct only certain specified expenses when computing the amount they are able to contribute to the support of a child being cared for at public expense is that the family
   A. should not be permitted to have a higher standard of living than the child being cared for
   B. the budget schedule is sufficiently generous and includes an allowance for other unusual expenses
   C. may not be able to verify their extraordinary expenses
   D. may meet other unusual expenses from the remainder of their surplus

3. Mrs. B. wishes to have her daughter, Mary, cared for at public expense. Her income includes her wages and OASDI benefits of $250 a month, of which $50 a month is paid for Mary and $50 a month for another minor member of the family who is already being cared for at public expense.
In order to determine the amount of Mrs. B.'s budget surplus, it is necessary to consider as income her wages and
   A. $50 of OASDI received for Mary
   B. $150 of the OASDI benefits
   C. $200 of the OASDI benefits
   D. $200 of the OASDI benefits if she is legally responsible for the care of the other child in placement

4. In order to determine a family's ability to contribute to the support of a child, the worker should
   A. have the legally responsible member sign Form W-279 agreeing to support the child, and then compute the family surplus on W-281 in accordance with public assistance standards
   B. compute the family's income in accordance with the allowance included on Form W-280 and the expenses included on Form W-279 and have Form W-279 signed if necessary
   C. use Form W-278 to work out a budget schedule for the family and compute their surplus on W-281 and then have them sign W-279 if necessary
   D. compute income and expenses on Form W-281, based on Form W-280, and have Form W-279 signed if necessary

Questions 5-10.

DIRECTIONS: Questions 5 through 10 are to be answered SOLELY on the basis of the following passage.

Too often in the past, society has accepted the existing social welfare programs, preferring to tinker with refinements when fundamental reform was in order. It has been a demeaning degrading welfare system in which the instrument of government was wrongfully and ineptly used. It has been a system which has only alienated those forced to benefit from it and demoralized those who had to administer it at the level where the pain was clearly visible.

There is a need to put this nation on a course in which cash benefits, providing a basic level of support, are conferred in such a way as to intrude as little as possible into privacy and self-respect. It is difficult to define a basic level of support, no matter how high or low it might be set. In the end, however, the design is not determined so much by how much is truly adequate for a family to meet all of its needs, but by the resources available to carry out the promise. That may be a harsh fact of life but it is also just that—a fact of life

5. Of the following, the MOST suitable title for the above passage would be
   A. THE NEED FOR GOVERNMENT CONTROL OF WELFARE
   B. DETERMINING THE BASIC LEVEL OF SUPPORT
   C. THE NEED FOR WELFARE REFORM
   D. THE ELIMINATION OF WELFARE PROGRAMS

6. In the above passage, the author's GREATEST criticism of the welfare system is that it is too
   A. disrespectful of recipients
   B. expensive to administer
   C. limited by regulations
   D. widespread in application

7. According to the above passage, the BASIC level of support is actually determined by
   A. how much is required for a family to meet all of its needs
   B. the age of the recipients
   C. how difficult it is to administer the program
   D. the economic resources of the nation

8. In the above passage, the author does NOT argue for
   A. a work incentive system
   B. a basic level of support
   C. cash benefits
   D. the privacy of recipients

9. As used in the above passage, the underlined word demeaning means MOST NEARLY
   A. ineffective
   B. expensive
   C. overburdened
   D. humiliating

10. As used in the above passage, the underlined word ineptly means MOST NEARLY
    A. foolishly
    B. unsuccessfully
    C. unskillfully
    D. unhappily

Questions 11-14.

DIRECTIONS: Questions 11 through 14 are to be answered SOLELY on the basis of the following paragraph.

The employment rate, which counts those unemployed in the sense that they are actively looking for work and unable to find it, gives a relatively superficial index of economic conditions in a community. A better index is the subemployment rate which includes the unemployment rate and also includes those working part-time while they are trying to get full-time work; those heads of households under 65 years of age who earn less than $240 per week working full-time, and those individuals under 65 who are not heads of households and earn less than $224 per week in a full-time job; and an estimate of the males *not counted*, which is a very real concern in ghetto areas.

11. Of the following, the MOST suitable title for the above paragraph would be
    A. EMPLOYMENT IN THE UNITED STATES
    B. PART-TIME WORKERS AND THE ECONOMY
    C. THE LABOR MARKET AND THE COMMUNITY
    D. TWO INDICATORS OF ECONOMIC CONDITIONS

12. On the basis of the above paragraph, which of the following statements is CORRECT?   12.____
    A. The unemployment rate includes everyone who is not fully employed.
    B. The subemployment rate is higher than the unemployment rate.
    C. The unemployment rate gives a more complete picture of the economic situation than the subemployment rate.
    D. The subemployment rate indicates how many part-time workers are dissatisfied with the number of hours they work per week.

13. As used in the above paragraph, the underlined word superficial means MOST NEARLY   13.____
    A. exaggerated   B. official   C. surface   D. current

14. According to the above paragraph, which of the following is included in the subemployment rate?   14.____
    A. Everyone who is unemployed
    B. All part-time workers
    C. Everyone under 65 who earns less than $220 per week in a full-time job
    D. All heads of households who earn less than $240 per week in a full-time job

Questions 15-16.

DIRECTIONS: Questions 15 and 16 are to be answered SOLELY on the basis of the following paragraphs.

The city's economy has its own dynamics, and there is only so much the government can do to shape it. But that margin is critically important. If the city uses its points of leverage, it can generate a large number of jobs—and good jobs, jobs that lead to advancement.

As a major employer itself, the city can upgrade the jobs it offers and greatly improve its services to the public if it does so. Since highly skilled professionals will always be in short supply, the city must train more paraprofessionals to take over routine tasks. Equally important, it must provide them with a realistic job ladder so they can move on up—nurse's aide to certified nurse, for example, teacher's aide to teacher. The training programs for such upgrading will require a substantial public investment but the cost-benefit return should be excellent.

As a major purchaser of goods and services, the city can stimulate business enterprise in the ghetto. The growth of Blacks and Puerto Rican firms will produce more local jobs; it will also create the kind of managerial talent the ghetto needs.

New kinds of enterprise can be set up. In housing, for example, there is a huge backlog of rehabilitation work to be done and a large pool of unskilled manpower to be trained for it. Corporations can be formed to take over tenements, remodel, and operate them, as in the Brownsville Home Maintenance Program. Grocery cooperatives to bring food prices down are another possibility.

15. According to the above paragraphs, the city is the major employer and by using its capacity it can
    A. assist unskilled people with talent to move up on the job ladder
    B. create private enterprises that will renew all areas of the city in need of renewal
    C. eliminate poverty in the ghetto areas by selective purchase of goods and services
    D. have no influence on the economy of the city

15.____

16. According to the above paragraph, one may REASONABLY conclude that
    A. the city has no power to influence the job market
    B. a byproduct of strategic purchasing and employment and training practices can be the rehabilitation of housing and the lowering of food prices
    C. highly skilled professions, which are now in short supply, will no longer be needed after paraprofessionals are trained to take over routine jobs
    D. the city's major objective is to bring down food prices

16.____

Questions 17-21.

DIRECTIONS: Questions 17 through 21 are to be answered SOLELY on the basis of the following paragraphs.
For each question, there are two statements.
Based on the information in the paragraphs, mark your answer:
A. If only statement is correct;
B. If only statement 2 is correct;
C. If both statements are correct;
D. if the excerpt do not contain sufficient evidence for concluding whether either or both statements are correct.

Upstate, 35% of the AFDC families lived in districts suburban to New York City, 43% in upstate urban districts, and 22% in the rest of upstate. Among white families, 28% resided in suburban districts, 40% in upstate urban districts, and 32% in the rest of upstate. Among non-white families, 43% lived in suburban districts, 47% in upstate urban districts, and 10% in the rest of upstate.

Upstate, 78.7% of the AFDC families resided in SMSA (Standard Metropolitan Statistical Area) counties, including 68.7% of the whites and 90.4% of the non-whites. In Buffalo, 83.3% of the families were non-white; in Rochester, 57.9% were non-whites; in cities of 100,000 to 250,000 (Albany, Syracuse, and Utica), 55.2% were white; and the rest of the upstate urban counties, 86.5% were white.

The two most frequent underlying reasons for a family requiring AFDC were desertion of the father (31.3% of the cases) and *father not married to mother* (30.%). Desertions were proportionately highest among Puerto Rican families (38.6%), compared with 29.4% for Blacks and 23.6% for white families. Unmarried mothers comprised 39.4% of the Black cases, compared with 26.6% for Puerto Ricans and 14.8% for white cases.

White families had substantially higher proportions in the separated and divorce categories than non-whites. When the deserted, separated, and divorced categories are combined, marital breakdown occurred in 59% of the white AFDC families, compared with 52.3% for Puerto Ricans and 44.4% for Blacks.

Substantial ethnic differences existed in the proportions of incapacitated fathers; overall, the rate was 7.5%, but among white families the rate was 14.8%, compared with 9.4% for Puerto Ricans and only 3.0% for Blacks. Families where the father was deceased comprised 5.9% of the AFDC cases.

In New York City, desertion rates (35.3% of all cases) were substantially higher than upstate (18.9%), particularly among white families, as ethnic differences in New York City diminished considerably. Unmarried mother rates closely paralleled the statewide figures.

Incapacity of the father occurred more frequently among white families upstate (17.5%) than among white families in New York City (104%). Deceased fathers were proportionately highest among the New York City Black and Puerto Rican caseload, possibly reflecting fewer remarriage and employment opportunities among these groups in the event of the death of the father.

17.   1.   The most frequent underlying reason for a family requiring AFDC was *father not married to mother*.   17.____
     2.   Three-fourths of New York State's AFDC families lived in New York City.

18.   1.   There were more cases of desertion among AFDC cases upstate than there were of incapacity of the father among white AFDC families upstate.   18.____
     2.   There was a higher percentage of marital breakdowns among white AFDC families compared to Puerto Rican for Black families.

19.   1.   Desertion of the father accounted for more AFDC cases than all other reasons combined.   19.____
     2.   The proportion of incapacitated fathers in Puerto Rican families was higher than the overall rate of incapacitated fathers.

20.   1.   Non-white families had substantially higher proportions in the divorced and separated categories than white families.   20.____
     2.   Among AFDC families in New York State, there were more Puerto Ricans than Blacks in the combined deserted, separated, and divorced categories

21.   1.   In New York City, there was a higher percentage of unmarried mothers among Puerto Rican AFDC families than among white cases.   21.____
     2.   Among white families, desertion rates were considerably higher upstate than in New York City.

Questions 22-25.

DIRECTIONS: Questions 22 through 25 are to be answered SOLELY on the basis of the information in the following paragraph.

The question of what material is relevant is not as simple as it might seem. Frequently, material which seems irrelevant to the inexperienced has, because of the common tendency to disguise and distort and misplace one's feelings, considerable significance. It may be necessary to let the client *ramble on* for a while in order to clear the decks, as it were, so that he may get down to things that really are on his mind. On the other hand, with an already disturbed person, it may be important for the interviewer to know when to discourage further elaboration of upsetting material. This is especially the case where the worker would be unable to do anything about it. An inexperienced interviewer might, for instance, be intrigued with the bizarre elaboration of material that the psychotic produces, but further elaboration of this might encourage the client in his instability. A too random discussion may indicate that the interviewee is not certain in what areas the interviewer is prepared to help him, and he may be seeking some direction. Or again, satisfying though it may be for the interviewer to have the interviewee tell him intimate details, such revelations sometimes need to be checked or encouraged only in small doses. An interviewee who has *talked too much* often reveals subsequent anxiety. This is illustrated by the fact that frequently after a *confessional* interview, the interviewee surprises the interviewer by being withdrawn, inarticulate, or hostile, or by breaking the next appointment.

22. Sometimes a client may reveal certain personal information to an interviewer and subsequently may feel anxious about this revelation.
    If, during an interview, a client begins to discuss very personal matters, it would be BEST to
    A. tell the client, in no uncertain terms, that you're not interested in personal details
    B. ignore the client at this point
    C. encourage the client to elaborate further on the details
    D. inform the client that the information seems to be very personal

23. The author indicates that clients with severe psychological disturbances pose an especially difficult problem for the inexperienced interviewer.
    The DIFFICULTY lies in the possibility of the client
    A. becoming physically violent and harming the interviewer
    B. rambling on for a while
    C. revealing irrelevant details which may be followed by cancelled appointments
    D. reverting to an unstable state as a result of interview material

24. An interviewer should be constantly alert to the possibility of obtaining clues from the client as to the problem areas.
    According to the above passage, a client who discusses topics at random may be
    A. unsure of what problems the interviewer can provide help
    B. reluctant to discuss intimate details
    C. trying to impress the interviewer with his knowledge
    D. deciding what relevant material to elaborate on

25. The evaluation of a client's responses may reveal substantial information that may aid the interviewer in assessing the problem areas that are of concern to the client. Responses that seemed irrelevant at the time of the interview may be of significance because
    A. considerable significance is attached to all irrelevant material
    B. emotional feelings are frequently masked
    C. an initial rambling on is often a prelude to what is actually bothering the client
    D. disturbed clients often reveal subsequent anxiety

25._____

KEY (CORRECT ANSWERS)

1.	C		11.	D
2.	D		12.	B
3.	B		13.	C
4.	D		14.	C
5.	C		15.	A
6.	A		16.	B
7.	D		17.	D
8.	A		18.	C
9.	D		19.	B
10.	C		20.	D

21. A
22. D
23. D
24. A
25. B

ARITHMETICAL REASONING
EXAMINATION SECTION
TEST 1

DIRECTIONS: Each question or incomplete statement is followed by several suggested answers or completions. Select the one that BEST answers the question or completes the statement. *PRINT THE LETTER OF THE CORRECT ANSWER IN THE SPACE AT THE RIGHT.*

1. On January 1, a family was receiving supplementary monthly public assistance of $280 for food, $240 for rent, and $140 for other necessities. In the spring, their rent rose by 10%, and their rent allotment was adjusted accordingly. In the summer, due to the death of a family member, their allotments for food and other necessities were reduced by 1/7.
   Their monthly allowance check in the fall should be
   A. $623   B. $644   C. $664   D. $684

2. Twice a month, a certain family receives a $340 general allowance for rent, food, and clothing expense. In addition, the family receives a specific supplementary allotment for utilities of $384 a year, which is added to their semi-monthly check.
   If the general allowance alone is reduced by 5%, what will be the TOTAL amount of their next semi-monthly check?
   A. $323   B. $339   C. $340   D. $355

3. If each supervising clerk in a certain unit sees an average of 9 clients in a 7-hour day and there are 15 supervising clerks in the unit, APPROXIMATELY how many clients will be seen in a 35-hour week?
   A. 315   B. 405   C. 675   D. 945

4. In one day, an aide receives 18 inquiries by phone and 27 inquiries in person. What percentage of the inquiries received that day were by phone?
   A. 33%   B. 40%   C. 45%   D. 60%

5. If the weekly paychecks for 5 employees are $258.64, $325.48, $287.50, and $313.12, then the combined weekly income for the 5 employee is
   A. $1,455.68   B. $1,456.08   C. $1,462.68   D. $1,474.08

6. Suppose that there are 17 aides working in an office where many community complaints are received by telephone. In one ten-day period, 4,250 calls were received.
   If the same number of calls were received each day and the aides divided the work load equally, about how many calls did each aide respond to daily?
   A. 25   B. 35   C. 75   D. 250

7. Suppose that an assignment was divided among 5 aides.
If the first aide spent 67 hours on the assignment, the second aide spent 95 hours, the third aide spent 52 hours, the fourth aide spent 78 hours, and the fifth aide spent 103 hours, what was the AVERAGE amount of time spent by each aide on the assignment? _____ hours.
   A. 71 B. 75 C. 79 D. 83

8. If there are 240 employees in a center and 1/3 are absent on the day of a bad snowstorm, how many employees were at work in the center on that day?
   A. 80 B. 120 C. 160 D. 200

9. Suppose that an aide takes 25 minutes to prepare a letter to a client.
If the aide is assigned to prepare 9 letters on a certain day, how much time should be set aside for this task? _____ hours.
   A. 3¾ B. 4¼ C. 4¾ D. 5¼

10. Suppose that a certain center uses both Form A and Form B in the course of its daily work and that Form A is used 4 times as often as Form B.
If the total number of both forms used in one week is 750, how many times was Form A used?
    A. 100 B. 200 C. 400 D. 600

11. Suppose a center has a budget of $2,185.40 from which 8 desks costing $156.10 apiece must be bought.
How many additional desks can be ordered from this budget after the 8 desks have been purchased?
    A. 4 B. 6 C. 9 D. 14

12. When researching a particular case, a team of 16 aides was asked to check through 234 folders to obtain the necessary information.
If half the aides worked twice as fast as the other half, and the slow group checked through 12 folders each hour, about how long would it take to complete the assignment? _____ hours.
    A. 4¼ B. 5 C. 6 D. 6½

13. The difference in the cost of two typewriters is $56.64.
If the less expensive typewriter costs $307.22, what is the cost of the other typewriter?
    A. $343.86 B. $344.06 C. $363.86 D. $364.06

14. At the start of a year, a family was receiving a public assistance grant of $382 twice a month, on the first and fifteenth of each month. On March 1, their rent allowance was decreased from $150 to $142 a month since they had moved to a smaller apartment. On August 1 their semi-monthly food allowance, which had been $80.40, was raised by 10%.
In that year, the TOTAL amount of money disbursed to this family was
    A. $4,544.20 B. $6,581.40 C. $9,088.40 D. $9,168.40

15. It is discovered that a client has received double public assistance for 2 months by having been enrolled at two service centers of the Department of Social Services. The client should have received $168 twice a month instead of the double amount. He now agrees to repay the money by equal deductions from his public assistance check over a period of 12 months.
    What will the amount of his NEXT check be?
    A. $112   B. $140   C. $154   D. $160

16. Suppose a study is being made of the composition of 3,550 families receiving public assistance. Of the first 1,050 families reviewed, 18% had four or more children.
    If, in the remaining number of families, the percentage with four or more children is half as high as the percentage in the group already reviewed, then the percentage of families with four or more children in the entire group of families is MOST NEARLY
    A. 12   B. 14   C. 16   D. 17

17. Suppose that food prices have risen 13%, and an increase of the same amount has been granted in the food allotment given to people receiving public assistance.
    If a family has been receiving $810 a month, 35% of which is allotted for food, then the TOTAL amount of public assistance this family receives per month will be changed to
    A. $805.42   B. $840.06   C. $846.86   D. $899.42

18. Assume that the food allowance is to be raised 5% in August but will be retroactive for four months to April.
    The retroactive allowance is to be divided into equal sections and added to the public assistance checks for August, September, October, November, and December.
    A family which has been receiving $840 monthly, 40% of which was allotted for food, will receive what size check in August?
    A. $853.44   B. $856.80   C. $861.00   D. $870.24

19. A blind client, who receives $210 public assistance twice a month, inherits 14 shares of stock worth $180 each. The client is required to sell the stock and spend his inheritance before receiving more public assistance.
    Using his public assistance allowance as a guide, how many months are his new assets expected to last?
    A. 6   B. 7   C. 8   D. 12

20. The Department of Social Services has 16 service centers. These centers may be divided into those which are downtown and those which are uptown. Two of the centers are special service centers and are downtown, while the remainder of the centers are general service centers. There is a total of 7 service centers downtown.
    The percentage of the general service centers which are uptown is MOST NEARLY
    A. 56   B. 64   C. 69   D. 79

21. For six months, a family lived in a 4-room apartment where they paid $380 a month. They made an intrasite move to a 4-room apartment where they paid $85 per room a month for six months.
Comparing the two six-month periods, the TOTAL amount of money the family saved by making the intrasite was
A. $240   B. $290   C. $430   D. $590

22. To calculate a tenant's usable income, you should make Social Security deductions of 4.4 percent on salary up to a maximum of $9,000 and State Disability deductions of .5 percent on salary up to $3,000.
What does a tenant's combined deduction amount to if his annual salary is $13,400?
A. $411.00   B. $568.60   C. $619.60   D. $700.00

23. If the temporary relocation expenses for housing are set at $18 per day for one adult and $10 per day for each additional person in a room, how much money is allowed for a woman and four children temporarily relocated in one room for a period of six days?
A. $168   B. $348   C. $378   D. $518

24. According to relocation policy, a family relocating to private housing from federally-aided or certain other sites will be granted a relocation payment. This payment equals the difference between 1/5 of the family's yearly income and the scheduled yearly rent for a standard apartment for their size family.
Suppose a 2-person family whose yearly income is $12,900 has been unable to obtain public housing and so finds a one-bedroom private apartment. The scheduled rent for a one-bedroom apartment appropriate for their occupancy is $240 a month.
What payment will they receive?
A. $240   B. $288   C. $300   D. $410

25. A family on a housing relocation site is paying $410 per month for rent. This represents 25% of their gross monthly income.
If the husband earns 4/5 of their total combined monthly income, how much does the wife earn per month?
A. $328   B. $540   C. $1,280   D. $1,500

KEY (CORRECT ANSWERS)

1.	A		11.	B
2.	B		12.	D
3.	C		13.	C
4.	B		14.	D
5.	B		15.	B
6.	A		16.	A
7.	C		17.	C
8.	C		18.	D
9.	A		19.	A
10.	D		20.	B

21. A
22. A
23. B
24. C
25. A

6 (#1)

SOLUTIONS TO PROBLEMS

1. After spring, the rent allotment should be $(240+24) = $264. After the summer, the reduced allotment for food and other necessities should be $[(280+140) − 1/7(280+140)] = $(420-1/7(420)] = $(420-60) = $360. The monthly check in the fall including rent, food, and other necessities should be $360 + $264 = $624.

2. Amount of general allowance in the family's semi-monthly check = $340. Amount of utilities allotment in the family's semi-monthly check: ($$\frac{384}{12}$ × ½) = $16. Amount of general allowance in family' semi-monthly check after a 5% reduction = $340 less 5% of $340 = $(340-17) = $3223. Total amount of the next month's semi-monthly check: Reduced general allowance + utilities allotment = $323 + $16 = $339.

3. During 7 hours, a total of (15)(9) = 135 clients can be seen. Thus, in 35 hours, a total of (135)(5) = 675 clients will be seen.

4. 18(18+27) = .40 = 40%

5. $258.64 + $325.48 + $287.34 + $271.50 + $313.12 = $1,456.08

6. 4250/10 = 425 calls per day. Then, 425/17 = 25

7. (67+95+52+78+103)/5 = 79 hours

8. Number present = (240)(2/3) = 160

9. (25)(9) = 225 min. = 3 hrs. 45 min. = 3 ¾ hours

10. Let x, 1/4x = number of forms A, B, respectively. Then, x + 1/4x = 750. Solving, x = 600

11. $2,185.40 − (8)($156.10) = $936.60. Then, $936.60 ÷ $156.10 = 6 desks

12. Since the slow group did 12 folders each hour, the faster group did 24 folders each hour. Then, 234/(12+24) = 6 ½ hrs.

13. Expensive typewriter costs $307.22 + $56.64 = $363.86

14. For months of January and February, the amount the family receives is $(382×2×2) = $1528
    For months of March through July, the family receives $(764-8) × 5 = $3780
    For months August through December, the family receives $(756+16.08) × 5 = $3860.40
    The total amount of money disbursed to this family is $1528 + $3780 + $3860.40 = $9,168.40

15. The overpayment for 2 months = ($168)(4) = $672. If this is paid back over 12 months, each month's amount is reduced by $672/12 = $56. Then, each check (semi-monthly) is reduced by $28. His next check will be $168 - $28 = $140

7 (#1)

16. $(1050)(.18) + (2500)(.09) = 414$. Then, $414/3550 = 12\%$

17. $(\$810)(.35) = \$283.50$ originally allotted for food. The new food allotment = $(\$283.50)(1.13) = \$320.355$. The total assistance now = $\$810 - \$283.50 + \$320.355 = \$846.855$ or $\$846.86$

18. $(\$840)(.40) = \$336$ per month for food. The new food allowance = $(\$336)(1.05) = \$352.80$ per month. The difference of $16.80 is retroactive to April, which means $(\$16.80)(9) = \$151.20$ additional money for August through December. Each check for these 5 months will be increased by $15.20/5 = 30.24$. Thus, the check in August = $840 + 30.24 = $840 + 30.24 = $870.24

19. $(\$180)(14) = \$2520$. Then, $\$2520/\$420 = 6$ months

20. 5 general are downtown; 9 of 14 general are uptown; $9/14 \approx 64\%$

21. $(\$85)(4) = \$340$ per month. Savings per month = $380 - $340 = $40 For six months, the savings = $240

22. $(\$9000)(.044) + (\$3000)(.005) = \$411$ total deductions

23. $(\$18+\$40)(6) = \$348$ relocation expenses

24. $(\$240)(12) - (1/5)(\$12,900) = \$300$ relocation payment

25. $\$410 \div .25 = \$1640$. The wife earns $(1640)(1/5) = \$328$ each month

---

TEST 2

DIRECTIONS: Each question or incomplete statement is followed by several suggested answers or completions. Select the one that BEST answers the question or completes the statement. *PRINT THE LETTER OF THE CORRECT ANSWER IN THE SPACE AT THE RIGHT.*

1. A project tenant who owns and drives a taxicab for living, reports for a three-month period an income of $6,250 after operating expenses of $1,300 have been considered. In addition, his tips are valued at 12% of his income before operating expenses.
   An estimate of his yearly income is MOST NEARLY
   A. $22,000   B. $23,000   C. $28,000
   D. $28,500   E. $29,000

   1.____

2. The maximum annual subsidy which can be paid by the State toward the operation of any low-rent housing project is the sum of the annual interest on the total original loan or building the project and 1% of the portion of the loan actually spent.
   If the original loan for a project was $8,000,000 at 1¾% interest, but only $7,500,000 was actually spent, then the MAXIMUM annual subsidy is
   A. $140,000   B. $145,000   C. $215,000
   D. $220,000   E. $271,250

   2.____

3. In 2020, the cost of repairs and maintenance at a certain housing project was $5,589 more than in 2019, representing an increase of 4.6%. A further increase at the same rate was anticipated for 2021.
   The cost of repairs and maintenance in 2021 was MOST NEARLY
   A. $127,100
   B. $132,700
   C. $132,900
   D. $133,000
   E. an amount which cannot be determined from the given data

   3.____

4. Each day a delivery truck used by the Housing Authority travels 25 miles from a project to a storehouse and 25 miles on the return trip. It travels at the rate of 30 miles per hour going to the storehouse and at the rate of 20 miles per hour returning.
   The average rate, in miles per hour, for the roundtrip is MOST NEARLY
   A. 24
   B. 25
   C. 26
   D. the square root of 600
   E. an amount which cannot be determined from the given data

   4.____

5. A report on the first 6,000 applications for apartments in a certain project containing 1,400 apartments indicated that those who were ineligible fell into four categories: 2,800 ineligible for reason A, 600 ineligible for reason B, 1,200 ineligible for reason C, and 400 ineligible for reason D.

   5.____

If the same proportions continue for the remaining 21,500 applications, then the percentage of eligible applicants who can be given apartments in the project is MOST NEARLY
A. 25 B. 30 C. 33 D. 40 E. 60

6. The number of applications for apartments in low-rent housing projects was 40,000 in 2019. The number of applications increased 5% in 2020, and increased again in 2021 by 6% over the 2,000 total.
The percentage by which the 2021 figures exceed the 2019 figures is
A. 5.3 B. 6.0 C. 11.0 D. 11.3 E. 30.0

7. A rectangular lot, 75 feet by 11.0 feet, was purchased as part of a project site for $28,500.
The price per square foot of this lot is MOST NEARLY
A. $2.85 B. $3.45 C. $3.95 D. $30.00 E. $30.95

8. It has been estimated that 125 kilowatt-hours of electricity are used each month in one average Housing Authority apartment at a cost of 14.8 cents per kilowatt-hour.
On this basis, the total cost of the electricity used in one year in a project containing 1,400 apartments is MOST NEARLY
A. $20,000 B. $25,000 C. $200,000
D. $250,000 E. $2,000,000

9. The walls and ceilings of 20 rooms are to be painted with the same kind of paint, each room being 15 feet long, 12 feet wide, and 10 feet high. Each room contains two windows, each 3 feet by 6 feet, and a door 3 feet by 8 feet, which are not to be painted. One gallon of paint covers 400 square feet of surface.
The number of gallons of paint needed is MOST NEARLY
A. 33 B. 34 C. 35 D. 36 E. 75

10. A group of buildings is valued at $11,500,000. Assume that the cos of fire insurance for these buildings is 5.3 cents per $100 of valuation per year.
The cost of fire insurance for one year is MOST NEARLY
A. $600 B. $6,000 C. $20,000
D. $60,000 E. $2,000,000

11. Of the 15 employees in a certain unit, one-third earn $27,600 per year, three earn $32,600, one earns $46,400, and the rest earn $33,800.
The average salary of the employees of this unit is MOST NEARLY
A. $31,000 B. $32,000 C. $33,000 D. $34,000 E. $35,000

12. Four pieces, each 2'8½" long, are cut from a piece of pipe 16½' long.
The length of the remaining piece of pipe is
A. 6'8½" B. 6'10" C. 6'10³/₈" D. 6'11¹/₈" E. 9'9½"

3 (#2)

13. A tenant ears E dollars a month, spends S dollars a week, and saves the rest. The tenant's yearly savings can be expressed by
    A. 12(E-4S)   B. 12E – 52S   C. 12(E-S)
    D. 52(E-4S)   E. E - S

14. A unit of fifteen Housing Assistants has been assigned the job of interviewing applicants. Each interview takes 35 minutes, and an additional 10 minutes is needed for making entries and notes. The last interview each day is always scheduled so that it can be completed that day.
    The number of applicants who can be interviewed in a week, consisting of five 7-hour days, is MOST NEARLY
    A. 375   B. 525   C. 675   D. 700   E. 725

15. A review of the 14,000 applications for apartments in a certain project containing 1,200 apartments indicated that 4,800 applicants were eligible and 6,400 were ineligible. No decision could be reached on the remaining applications because certain necessary information was omitted by the applicants, but it was assumed that the proportion of eligible and ineligible applicants would remain the same as in those already decided.
    On the basis of these figures, the percentage of eligible applicants who can be given apartments in the project is
    A. under 17%   B. 17%   C. 20%
    D. 25%   E. 33 1/3%

16. An oil burner in a housing development burns 76 gallons of fuel oil per hour. At 9 A.M. on a very cold day, the superintendent asks the Housing Manager to put in an emergency order for more fuel oil. At that time, he reports that he has on hand 266 gallons. At noon, he again comes to the manager, notifying him that no oil has been delivered.
    The MAXIMUM amount of time that he can continue to furnish heat without receiving more oil is
    A. no more time   B. ½ hour   C. 1 hour
    D. 1½ hours   E. 2 hours

17. As a result of reports received by the Housing Authority concerning the reputed ineligibility of 756 tenants because of above-standard incomes, an intensive check of their employers has been ordered. Four housing assistants have been assigned to this task. At the end of 6 days at 7 hours each, they have checked on 336 tenants. In order to speed up the investigation, two more housing assistants are assigned to this point.
    If they worked at the same rate, the number of additional 7-hour days it would take to complete the job is MOST NEARLY
    A. 1   B. 3   C. 5   D. 7   E. 9

4 (#2)

18. A municipal aide on a special trip is returning to his office from a point 17½ miles away, and makes the return trip to his office at an average speed of 25 miles an hour, except for a 15-minute stopover at one point to get a flat tire fixed. The time it should take him to reach his office is MOST NEARLY _____ minutes.
    A. 12 B. 22 C. 36 D. 42 E. 57

19. A district office has an assigned staff of 320 employees. Of this number, 25% are not available for duty due to illness, vacations, and other reasons. Of those who are available for duty, 1/8 are assigned to auditing and special projects, and the rest to handling the workload.
    The ACTUAL number of employees available for handling the workload is
    A. 350 B. 310 C. 270 D. 210 E. 180

20. Two dozen shuttlecocks and four badminton rackets are to be purchased for a playground. The shuttlecocks are priced at $3.60 each, and the rackets at $27.50 each. The playground receives a discount of 30% from these prices.
    The TOTAL cost of this equipment is
    A. $72.90 B. $114.30 C. $137.48 D. $186.00 E. $220.70

21. On January 1, a family was receiving public assistance allowance of $185 for food, $53 for clothing, $17.50 for utilities, and $22 for personal needs, all semi-monthly, and a monthly allowance of $550 for rent. On May 1, the rent allowance was increased by 12% but all other allowances remained the same for the rest of the year.
    The TOTAL amount of money granted this family during the year was
    A. $10,528   B. $13,262   C. $13,788
    D. $21,056   E. $27,676

22. It has been decided to make changes in food allotments to clients receiving public assistance to conform to changes in food costs. Of the food allowance, 30% is intended for meat, 30% for fruits and vegetables, 25% for groceries, and 15% for dairy products. Assume that meat prices have gone up 5%, and dairy prices have remained the same.
    For a family that has been receiving $400 per month for food, the new monthly food allowance will be
    A. $333 B. $375 C. $393 D. $403.50 E. $420

23. On January 1, a family was receiving a public assistance allowance of $195 for food, $63 for clothing, $27.50 for utilities, and $32 for personal needs, all semi-monthly, and a monthly allowance of $510 for rent. On June 1, the rent allowance was increased by 12%, but all other allowances remained the same for the rest of the year.
    The TOTAL amount of money granted this family during the year was
    A. $13,843.40   B. $14,107.20   C. $14,168.40
    D. $14,474.40   E. $16,886.80

24. A member of a family receiving public assistance amounting to $600 monthly has obtained a part-time job, for which he is paid $40 a day. He is employed 3 days a week. His carfare costs $3.00 per day and his lunches $2.00 per day. Assume that there are $4^1/_3$ weeks per month. The Department of Welfare requires that net earnings be deducted from relief allowances.
The family's semi-monthly public assistance allowances should be reduced to
   A. $40.00   B. $72.50   C. $96.25   D. $123.75   E. $145.00

24.____

25. A couple living in a furnished room has been receiving a public assistance grant of $375 semi-monthly and has been paying a weekly rent of $75. The landlord has been granted a 12% increase in rent. Assume that a month consists of $4^1/_3$ weeks.
The amount of the new semi-monthly grant, including this rent increase, that the couple will receive will be MOST NEARLY
   A. $394.50   B. $397   C. $409   D. $514   E. $557

25.____

KEY (CORRECT ANSWERS)

1.	D		11.	B
2.	C		12.	A
3.	C		13.	B
4.	A		14.	C
5.	B		15.	C
6.	D		16.	B
7.	B		17.	C
8.	D		18.	E
9.	A		19.	D
10.	B		20.	C

      21.   C
      22.   C
      23.   C
      24.   B
      25.   A

SOLUTIONS TO PROBLEMS

1. For 3 months, income = $6,250 + (.12)($7550) = $7156. Then, annual income = ($7154)(4) = $28,624, closest to $28,500.

2. Maximum annual subsidy = ($8,000,000)(.0175) + (.01)($7,500,000) = $215,000

3. Cost in 2019 = $5589/.046 = $121,500. The cost in 2020 = $121,500 + $5589 = $127,089. This means the cost in 2021 = ($127,089)(1.046) = $132,900

4. Average rate = total distance/total time = (25+25) ÷ (25/30 + 25/20) = 24 mph

5. Out of 600, number of eligible = 6000 – 2800 – 600 – 1200 – 400 = 1000. Thus, for 27,500 applications, (1/6)(27,500) = 4583 would be eligible. Finally, 1400 ÷ 4583 ≈ 30%

6. Number of applications in 2020 = (40,000)(1.05) = 42,000. Number of applications in 2021 = (42,000)(1.06) = 44,520. Then, (44,520–40,000) ÷ 40,000 = 11.3%

7. $28,500 ÷ [(75×110)] = $3.45 per sq. ft.

8. Total cost = (125)(.148)(12)(1400) = $310,800; closest to choice D of $250,000

9. Painted area of each room = (2)(15)(10) + (2)(12)(10) + (15)(12) – (2)(3)(6) – (3)(8) = 660 sq. ft. So, (20)(660) = 13,200 sq. ft. to be painted in all rooms. Finally, 13,200/400 = 33 gallons of paint needed

10. Insurance cost = (.053)($11,500,000)/$100 = $6095, closest to $6000

11. [(5)($27,600) + (3)($32,600) + (1)($46,400) + (6)($33,800)]/15 = $32,233 closest to $32,000

12. 16½ - (4)(2'5³⁄₈") = 16'6" – 8'21½" = 16'6" – 9'9½" = 6'8½"

13. Annual savings = 12E – 52S

14. 7 ÷ ¾ = 9.$\bar{3}$, which means each interviewer can interview a maximum of 9 applicants each day. Then, (5)(9)(15) = 675 applicants

15. 4800/(4800+6400) = 3/7 eligible. On that assumption, there would be (3/7)(14,000) = 6000 eligible applicants. Then, 1200/6000 = 20%

16. 266 – (3)(76) = 38 gallons of oil left. Then, 38/76 = ½ hour

17. (6)(7)(4) = 168 hours to check on 336 tenants. This means 2 tenants require 1 man-hour. Now, (6)(7)(x days) = man-hours would be needed to check the remaining 420 tenants. This requires 210 man-hours. So, (6)(7)(x) = 210. Solving, x = 5

18. $\frac{17.5}{25}$ = .7 hr. = 42 min. Total time = 42 + 15 = 57 minutes.

19. Number available = $320[1-.25(1/8)(.75)] = 210$

20. Total cost = $(.70)[(24)(\$3.60)+(4)(27.50)] = \$137.48$

21. From January through April, amount = $(8)(\$185+\$53+\$17.50+\$22) + (4)(\$550) = \$4420$. From May through December, amount = $(16)(\$185+\$53+17.50+\$22) + (8)(\$550)(1.12) = \$9368$. Total annual amount = $\$4420 + \$9368 = \$13,788$

22. Meat allowance = $(\$400)(.30)(1.10) = \$132$; fruit and vegetable allowance = $(\$400)(.30)(.80) = \$96$; grocery allowance = $(\$400)(.25)(1.05) = \$105$; dairy allowance = $(\$400)(.15) = \$60$. New monthly allowance = $\$132 + \$96 + \$105 + \$.60 = \$393$

23. From January through May, amount = $(10)(\$195+\$63+\$27.50+\$32) + (5)(\$510) = \$5725$. From June through December, amount = $(14)(\$195+\$63+\$27.50+\$32) + (7)(\$510)(1.12) = \$8443.40$. Total annual amount = $\$5725 + \$8443.40 = \$14,168.40$

24. Monthly assistance should be reduced to $\$600 - [(40)(3)(4^1/_3) - (\$5)(3)(4^1/_3)] = \$145$. So, the semi-monthly amount is now $\$145/2 = \$72.50$

25. $(\$75)(4^1/_3)/2$ = original semi-monthly rent.
New semi-monthly rent = $(162.50)(1.12) = \$182$. Since this represents an increase of $\$19.50$, the new semi-monthly grant will be increased to $\$375 + \$19.50 = \$394.50$

PREPARING WRITTEN MATERIAL

PARAGRAPH REARRANGEMENT
COMMENTARY

The sentences that follow are in scrambled order. You are to rearrange them in proper order and indicate the letter choice containing the correct answer at the space at the right.

Each group of sentences in this section is actually a paragraph presented in scrambled order. Each sentence in the group has a place in that paragraph; no sentence is to be left out. You are to read each group of sentences and decide upon the best order in which to put the sentences so as to form a well-organized paragraph.

The questions in this section measure the ability to solve a problem when all the facts relevant to its solution are not given.

More specifically, certain positions of responsibility and authority require the employee to discover connection between events sometimes, apparently, unrelated. In order to do this, the employee will find it necessary to correctly infer that unspecified events have probably occurred or are likely to occur. This ability becomes especially important when action must be taken on incomplete information.

Accordingly, these questions require competitors to choose among several suggested alternatives, each of which presents a different sequential arrangement of the events. Competitors must choose the MOST logical of the suggested sequences.

In order to do so, they may be required to draw on general knowledge to infer missing concepts or events that are essential to sequencing the given events. Competitors should be careful to infer only what is essential to the sequence. The plausibility of the wrong alternatives will always require the inclusion of unlikely events or of additional chains of events which are NOT essential to sequencing the given events.

It's very important to remember that you are looking for the best of the four possible choices, and that the best choice of all may not even be one of the answers you're given to choose from.

There is no one right way to solve these problems. Many people have found it helpful to first write out the order of the sentences, as they would have arranged them, on their scrap paper before looking at the possible answers. If their optimum answer is there, this can save them some time. If it isn't, this method can still give insight into solving the problem. Others find it most helpful to just go through each of the possible choices, contrasting each as they go along. You should use whatever method feels comfortable and works for you.

While most of these types of questions are not that difficult, we've added a higher percentage of the difficult type, just to give you more practice. Usually there are only one or two questions on this section that contain such subtle distinctions that you're unable to answer confidently. And you then may find yourself stuck deciding between two possible choices, neither of which you're sure about.

EXAMINATION SECTION
TEST 1

DIRECTIONS: Each question consists of several sentences which can be arranged in a logical sequence. For each question, select the choice which places the numbered sentences in the MOST logical sequence. *PRINT THE LETTER OF THE CORRECT ANSWER IN THE SPACE AT THE RIGHT.*

1. I. A body was found in the woods.
   II. A man proclaimed innocence.
   III. The owner of a gun was located.
   IV. A gun was traced.
   V. The owner of a gun was questioned.
   The CORRECT answer is:
   A. IV, III, V, II, I
   B. II, I, IV, III, V
   C. I, IV, III, V, II
   D. I, III, V, II, IV
   E. I, II, IV, III, V

   1.____

2. I. A man is in a hunting accident.
   II. A man fell down a flight of steps.
   III. A man lost his vision in one eye.
   IV. A man broke his leg.
   V. A man had to walk with a cane.
   The CORRECT answer is:
   A. II, IV, V, I, III
   B. IV, V, I, III, II
   C. III, I, IV, V, II
   D. I, III, V, II, IV
   E. I, III, II, IV, V

   2.____

3. I. A man is offered a new job.
   II. A woman is offered a new job.
   III. A man works as a waiter.
   IV. A woman works as a waitress.
   V. A woman gives notice.
   The CORRECT answer is:
   A. IV, II, V, III, I
   B. IV, II, V, I, III
   C. II, IV, V, III, I
   D. III, I, IV, II, V
   E. IV, III, II, V, I

   3.____

4. I. A train let the station late.
   II. A man was late for work.
   III. A man lost his job.
   IV. Many people complained because the train was late.
   V. There was a traffic jam.
   The CORRECT answer is:
   A. V, II, I, IV, III
   B. V, I, IV, II, III
   C. V, I, II, IV, III
   D. I, V, IV, II, III
   E. II, I, IV, V, III

   4.____

5. I. The burden of proof as to each issue is determined before trial and remains upon the same party throughout the trial.
    II. The jury is at liberty to believe one witness' testimony as against a number of contradictory witnesses.
    III. In a civil case, the party bearing the burden of proof is required to prove his contention by a fair preponderance of the evidence.
    IV. However, it must be noted that a fair preponderance of evidence does not necessarily mean a greater number of witnesses.
    V. The burden of proof is the burden which rests upon one of the parties to an action to persuade the trier of the facts, generally the jury, that a proposition he asserts is true.
    VI. If the evidence is equally balanced, or if it leaves the jury in such doubt as to be unable to decide the controversy either way, judgment must be given against the party upon whom the burden of proof rests.
    The CORRECT answer is:
    A. III, II, V, IV, I, VI   B. I, II, VI, V, III, IV   C. III, IV, V, I, II, VI
    D. V, I, III, VI, IV, II   E. I, V, III, VI, IV, II

6. I. If a parent is without assets and is unemployed, he cannot be convicted of the crime of non-support of a child.
    II. The term *sufficient ability* has been held to mean sufficient financial ability.
    III. It does not matter if his unemployment is by choice or unavoidable circumstances.
    IV. If he fails to take any steps at all, he may be liable to prosecution for endangering the welfare of a child.
    V. Under the penal law, a parent is responsible for the support of his minor child only if the parent is of *sufficient ability*.
    VI. An indigent parent may meet his obligation by borrowing money or by seeking aid under the provisions of the Social Welfare Law.
    The CORRECT answer is:
    A. VI, I, V, III, II, IV   B. I, III, V, II, IV, VI   C. V, II, I, III, VI, IV
    D. I, VI, IV, V, II, III   E. II, V, I, III, VI, IV

7. I. Consider, for example, the case of a rabble rouser who urges a group of twenty people to go out and break the windows of a nearby factory.
    II. Therefore, the law fills the indicated gap with the crime of *inciting to riot*.
    III. A person is considered guilty of inciting to riot when he urges ten or more persons to engage in tumultuous and violent conduct of a kind likely to create public alarm.
    IV. However, if he has not obtained the cooperation of at least four people, he cannot be charged with unlawful assembly.
    V. The charge of inciting to riot was added to the law to cover types of conduct which cannot be classified as either the crime of *riot* or the crime of *unlawful assembly*.
    VI. If he acquires the acquiescence of at least four of them, he is guilty of unlawful assembly even if the project does not materialize.
    The CORRECT answer is:
    A. III, V, I, VI, IV, II   B. V, I, IV, VI, II, III   C. III, IV, I, V, II, VI
    D. V, I, IV, VI, III, II   E. V, III, I, VI, IV, II

8.
   I. If, however, the rebuttal evidence presents an issue of credibility, it is for the jury to determine whether the presumption has, in fact, been destroyed.
   II. Once sufficient evidence to the contrary is introduced, the presumption disappears from the trial.
   III. The effect of a presumption is to place the burden upon the adversary to come forward with evidence to rebut the presumption.
   IV. When a presumption is overcome and ceases to exist in the case, the fact or facts which gave rise to the presumption still remain.
   V. Whether a presumption has been overcome is ordinarily a question for the court.
   VI. Such information may furnish a basis for a logical inference.
   The CORRECT answer is:
   A. IV, VI, II, V, I, III   B. III, II, V, I, IV, VI   C. V, III, VI, IV, II, I
   D. V, IV, I, II, VI, III   E. II, III, V, I, IV, VI

   8.____

9.
   I. An executive may answer a letter by writing his reply on the face of the letter itself instead of having a return letter typed.
   II. This procedure is efficient because it saves the executive's time, the typist's time, and saves office file space.
   III. Copying machines are used in small offices as well as large offices to save time and money in making brief replies to business letters.
   IV. A copy is made on a copying machine to go into the company files, while the original is mailed back to the sender.
   The CORRECT answer is:
   A. I, II, IV, III   B. I, IV, II, III   C. III, I, IV, II   D. III, IV, II, I

   9.____

10.
    I. Most organizations favor one of the types but always include the others to a lesser degree.
    II. However, we can detect a definite trend toward greater use of symbolic control.
    III. We suggest that our local police agencies are today primarily utilizing material control.
    IV. Control can be classified into three types: physical, material, and symbolic.
    The CORRECT answer is:
    A. IV, II, III, I   B. II, I, IV, III   C. III, IV, II, I   D. IV, I, III, II

    10.____

11.
    I. Project residents had first claim to this use, followed by surrounding neighborhood children.
    II. By contrast, recreation space within the project's interior was found to be used more often by both groups.
    III. Studies of the use of project grounds in many cities showed grounds left open for public use were neglected and unused, both by residents and by members of the surrounding community.
    IV. Project residents had clearly laid claim to the play spaces, setting up and enforcing unwritten rules for use.
    V. Each group, by experience, found their activities easily disrupted by other groups, and their claim to the use of space for recreation difficult to enforce.

    11.____

The CORRECT answer is:
A. IV, V, I, II, III
B. V, II, IV, III, I
C. I, IV, III, II, V
D. III, V, II, IV, I

12. I. They do not consider the problems correctable within the existing subsidy formula and social policy of accepting all eligible applicants regardless of social behavior.
    II. A recent survey, however, indicated that tenants believe these problems correctable by local housing authorities and management within the existing financial formula.
    III. Many of the problems and complaints concerning public housing management and design have created resentment between the tenant and the landlord.
    IV. This same survey indicated that administrators and managers do not agree with the tenants.
    The CORRECT answer is:
    A. II, I, III, IV   B. I, III, IV, II   C. III, II, IV, I   D. IV, II, I, III

13. I. In single-family residences, there is usually enough distance between tenants to prevent occupants from annoying one another.
    II. For example, a certain small percentage of tenant families has one or more members addicted to alcohol.
    III. While managers believe in the right of individuals to live as they choose, the manager becomes concerned when the pattern of living jeopardizes others' rights.
    IV. Still others turn night into day, staging lusty entertainments which carry on into the hours when most tenants are trying to sleep.
    V. In apartment buildings, however, tenants live so closely together that any misbehavior can result in unpleasant living conditions.
    VI. Other families engage in violent argument.
    The CORRECT answer is:
    A. III, II, V, IV, VI, I
    B. I, V, II, VI, IV, III
    C. II, V, IV, I, III, VI
    D. IV, II, V, VI, III, I

14. I. Congress made the commitment explicit in the Housing Act of 194, establishing as a national goal the realization of a *decent home and suitable environment for every American family*.
    II. The result has been that the goal of decent home and suitable environment is still as far distant as ever for the disadvantaged urban family.
    III. In spite of this action by Congress, federal housing programs have continued to be fragmented and grossly underfunded.
    IV. The passage of the National Housing Act signaled a few federal commitment to provide housing for the nation's citizens.
    The CORRECT answer is:
    A. I, IV, III, II   B. IV, I, III, II   C. IV, I, II, III   D. II, IV, I, III

15.
 I. The greater expense does not necessarily involve *exploitation*, but it is often perceived as exploitative and unfair by those who are aware of the price differences involved, but unaware of operating costs.
 II. Ghetto residents believe they are *exploited* by local merchants, and evidence substantiates some of these beliefs.
 III. However, stores in low-income areas were more likely to be small independents, which could not achieve the economies available to supermarket chains and were, therefore, more likely to charge higher prices, and the customers were more likely to buy smaller-sized packages which are more expensive per unit of measure.
 IV. A study conducted in one city showed that distinctly higher prices were charged for goods sold in ghetto stores in other areas.
 The CORRECT answer is:
  A. IV, II, I, III   B. IV, I, III, II   C. II, IV, III, I   D. II, III, IV, I

KEY (CORRECT ANSWERS)

1.	C	6.	C	11.	D
2.	E	7.	A	12.	C
3.	B	8.	B	13.	B
4.	B	9.	C	14.	B
5.	D	10.	D	15.	C

PREPARING WRITTEN MATERIALS
EXAMINATION SECTION
TEST 1

DIRECTIONS: Each question consists of a sentence which may be classified appropriately under one of the following four categories:
  A. Incorrect because of faulty grammar or sentence structure;
  B. Incorrect because of faulty punctuation;
  C. Incorrect because of faulty capitalization;
  D. Correct

Examine each sentence carefully. Then, in the space at the right, indicate the letter preceding the category which is the BEST of the four suggested above. Each incorrect sentence contains only one type of error. Consider a sentence correct if it contains no errors, although there may be other correct ways of expressing the same thought.

1. All the employees, in this office, are over twenty-one years old.   1.____

2. Neither the clerk nor the stenographer was able to explain what had happened.   2.____

3. Mr. Johnson did not know who he would assign to type the order.   3.____

4. Mr. Marshall called her to report for work on Saturday.   4.____

5. He might of arrived on time if the train has not been delayed.   5.____

6. Some employees on the other hand, are required to fill out these forms every month.   6.____

7. The supervisor issued special instructions to his subordinates to prevent their making errors.   7.____

8. Our supervisor Mr. Williams, expects to be promoted in about two weeks.   8.____

9. We were informed that prof. Morgan would attend the conference.   9.____

10. The clerks were assigned to the old building; the stenographers, to the new building.   10.____

11. The supervisor asked Mr. Smith and I to complete the work as quickly as possible.   11.____

12. He said, that before an employee can be permitted to leave, the report must be finished.   12.____

13. A calculator, in addition to the three computers, are needed in the new office. 13._____

14. Having made many errs in her work, the supervisor asked the typist to be more careful. 14._____

15. "If you are given an assignment," he said, "you should begin work on it as quickly as possible." 15._____

16. All the clerks, including those who have been appointed recently are required to work on the new assignment. 16._____

17. The office manager asked each employee to work one Saturday a month. 17._____

18. Neither Mr. Smith nor Mr. Jones was able to finish his assignment on time. 18._____

19. The task of filing these cards is to be divided equally between you and he. 19._____

20. He is an employee whom we consider to be efficient. 20._____

21. I believe that the new employees are not as punctual as us. 21._____

22. The employees, working in this office, are to be congratulated for their work. 22._____

23. The delay in preparing the report was caused, in his opinion, by the lack of proper supervision and coordination. 23._____

24. John Jones accidentally pushed the wrong button and then all the lights went out. 24._____

25. The investigator ought to of had the witness sign the statement. 25._____

KEY (CORRECT ANSWERS)

1.	B		11.	A
2.	D		12.	B
3.	A		13.	A
4.	C		14.	A
5.	A		15.	D
6.	B		16.	B
7.	D		17.	C
8.	B		18.	D
9.	C		19.	A
10.	D		20.	D

21. A
22. B
23. D
24. D
25. A

TEST 2

Questions 1-10.

DIRECTIONS: Each of the following sentences may be classified under one of the following four options:
- A. Faulty; contains an error in grammar only
- B. Faulty; contains an error in spelling only
- C. Faulty; contains an error in grammar and an error in spelling
- D. Correct; contains no error in grammar or in spelling

Examine each sentence carefully to determine under which of the above four options it is BEST classified. Then, in the space at the right, write the letter preceding the option which is the best of the four listed above.

1. A recognized principle of good management is that an assignment should be given to whomever is best qualified to carry it out.   1.____

2. He considered it a privilege to be allowed to review and summarize the technical reports issued annually by your agency.   2.____

3. Because the warehouse was in an inaccessible location, deliveries of electric fixtures from the warehouse were made only in large lots.   3.____

4. Having requisitioned the office supplies, Miss Brown returned to her desk and resumed the computation of petty cash disbursements.   4.____

5. One of the advantages of this chemical solution is that records treated with it are not inflamable.   5.____

6. The complaint of this employee, in addition to the complaints of the other employees, were submitted to the grievance committee.   6.____

7. A study of the duties and responsibilities of each of the various categories of employees was conducted by an unprejudiced classification analyst.   7.____

8. Ties of friendship with this subordinate compels him to withold the censure that the subordinate deserves.   8.____

9. Neither of the agencies are affected by the decision to institute a program for rehabilitating physically handi-caped men and women.   9.____

10. The chairman stated that the argument between you and he was creating an intolerable situation.   10.____

2 (#2)

Questions 11-25.

DIRECTIONS: Each of the following sentences may be classified under one of the following four options:
    A. Correct
    B. Sentence contains an error in spelling
    C. Sentence contains an error in grammar
    D. Sentence contains errors in both grammar and spelling.

11. He reported that he had had a really good time during his vacation although the farm was located in a very inaccessible portion of the country.   11.____

12. It looks to me like he has been fasinated by that beautiful painting.   12.____

13. We have permitted these kind of pencils to accumulate on our shelves, knowing we can sell them at a profit of five cents apiece any time we choose.   13.____

14. Believing that you will want an unexagerated estimate of the amount of business we can expect, I have made every effort to secure accurate figures.   14.____

15. Each and every man, woman and child in that untrammeled wilderness carry guns for protection against the wild animals.   15.____

16. Although this process is different than the one to which he is accustomed, a good chemist will have no trouble.   16.____

17. Insensible to the fuming and fretting going on about him, the engineer continued to drive the mammoth dynamo to its utmost capacity.   17.____

18. Everyone had studied his lesson carefully and was consequently well prepared when the instructor began to discuss the fourth dimention.   18.____

19. I learned Johnny six new arithmetic problems this afternoon.   19.____

20. Athletics is urged by our most prominent citizens as the pursuit which will enable the younger generation to achieve that ideal of education, a sound mind in a sound body.   20.____

21. He did not see whoever was at the door very clearly but thinks it was the city tax appraiser.   21.____

22. He could not scarsely believe that his theories had been substantiated in this convincing fashion.   22.____

23. Although you have displayed great ingenuity in carrying out your assignments, the choice for the position still lies among Brown and Smith.   23.____

24. If they had have pleaded at the time that Smith was an accessory to the   24._____
    crime, it would have lessened the punishment.

25. It has proven indispensible in his compilation of the facts in the matter.   25._____

KEY (CORRECT ANSWERS)

1. A
2. D
3. B
4. D
5. B

6. A
7. D
8. C
9. C
10. A

11. A
12. D
13. C
14. B
15. D

16. C
17. A
18. B
19. C
20. A

21. B
22. D
23. C
24. D
25. B

TEST 3

Questions 1-5.

DIRECTIONS: Questions 1 through 5 consist of sentences which may or may not contain errors in grammar or spelling or both. Sentences which do not contain errors in grammar or spelling or both are to be considered correct, even though there may be other correct ways of expressing the same thought. Examine each sentence carefully. Then, in the space at the right, write the letter of the answer which is the BEST of those suggested below.
- A. If the sentence is correct
- B. If the sentence contains an error in spelling
- C. If the sentence contains an error in grammar
- D. If the sentence contains errors in both grammar and spelling.

1. Brown is doing fine although the work is irrevelant to his training. 1.____

2. The conference of sales managers voted to set its adjournment at one o'clock in order to give those present an opportunity to get rid of all merchandise. 2.____

3. He decided that in view of what had taken place at the hotel that he ought to stay and thank the benificent stranger who had rescued him from an embarassing situation. 3.____

4. Since you object to me criticizing your letter, I have no alternative but to consider you a mercenary scoundrel. 4.____

5. I rushed home ahead of schedule so that you will leave me go to the picnic with Mary. 5.____

Questions 6-15.

DIRECTIONS: Some of the following sentences contain an error in spelling, word usage, or sentence structure, or punctuation. Some sentences are correct as they stand although there may be other correct ways of expressing the same thought. All incorrect sentences contain only one error. Mark your answer to each question in the space at the right as follows:
- A. If the sentence has an error in spelling
- B. If the sentence has an error in punctuation or capitalization
- C. If the sentence has an error in word usage or sentence structure
- D. If the sentence is correct

6. Because the chairman failed to keep the participants from wandering off into irrelevant discussions, it was impossible to reach a consensus before the meeting was adjourned. 6.____

7. Certain employers have an unwritten rule that any applicant, who is over 55 years of age, is automatically excluded from consideration for any position whatsoever. 7.____

8. If the proposal to build schools in some new apartment buildings were to be accepted by the builders, one of the advantages that could be expected to result would be better communication between teachers and parents of schoolchildren.   8.____

9. In this instance, the manufacturer's violation of the law against deseptive packaging was discernible only to an experienced inspector.   9.____

10. The tenants' anger stemmed from the president's going to Washington to testify without consulting them first.   10.____

11. Did the president of this eminent banking company say; "We intend to hire and train a number of these disadvantaged youths?"   11.____

12. In addition, today's confidential secretary must be knowledgable in many different areas: for example, she must know modern techniques for making travel arrangements for the executive.   12.____

13. To avoid further disruption of work in the offices, the protesters were forbidden from entering the building unless they had special passes.   13.____

14. A valuable secondary result of our training conferences is the opportunities afforded for management to observe the reactions of the participants.   14.____

15. Of the two proposals submitted by the committee, the first one is the best.   15.____

Questions 16-25.

DIRECTIONS: Each of the following sentences may be classified MOST appropriately under one of the following three categories:
  A. Faulty because of incorrect grammar
  B. Faulty because of incorrect punctuation
  C. Correct

Examine each sentence. Then, print the capital letter preceding the BEST choice of the three suggested above. All incorrect sentences contain only one type of error. Consider a sentence correct if it contains none of the types of errors mentioned, even though there may be other ways of expressing the same thought.

16. He sent the notice to the clerk who you hired yesterday.   16.____

17. It must be admitted, however that you were not informed of this change.   17.____

18. Only the employees who have served in this grade for at least two years are eligible for promotion.   18.____

19. The work was divided equally between she and Mary.   19.____

3 (#3)

20. He thought that you were not available at that time. 20.____
21. When the messenger returns; please give him this package. 21.____
22. The new secretary prepared, typed, addressed, and delivered, the notices. 22.____
23. Walking into the room, his desk can be seen at the rear. 23.____
24. Although John has worked here longer than she, he produces a smaller amount of work. 24.____
25. She said she could of typed this report yesterday. 25.____

KEY (CORRECT ANSWERS)

1.	D	11.	B
2.	A	12.	A
3.	D	13.	C
4.	C	14.	D
5.	C	15.	C
6.	A	16.	A
7.	B	17.	B
8.	D	18.	C
9.	A	19.	A
10.	D	20.	C
21.	B		
22.	B		
23.	A		
24.	C		
25.	A		

TEST 4

Questions 1-5.

DIRECTIONS: Each of the following sentences may be classified MOST appropriately under one of the following three categories:
- A. Faulty because of incorrect grammar
- B. Faulty because of incorrect punctuation
- C. Correct

Examine each sentence. Then, print the capital letter preceding the BEST choice of the three suggested above. All incorrect sentences contain only one type of error. Consider a sentence correct if it contains none of the types of errors mentioned, even though there may be other ways of expressing the same thought.

1. Neither one of these procedures are adequate for the efficient performance of this task.   1.____

2. The keyboard is the tool of the typist; the cash register, the tool of the cashier.   2.____

3. "The assignment must be completed as soon as possible" said the supervisor.   3.____

4. As you know, office handbooks are issued to all new employees.   4.____

5. Writing a speech is sometimes easier than to deliver it before an audience.   5.____

Questions 6-15.

DIRECTIONS: Each statement given in Questions 6 through 15 contains one of the faults of English usage listed below. For each, choose from the options listed the MAJOR fault contained.
- A. The statement is not a complete sentence.
- B. The statement contains a word or phrase that is redundant.
- C. The statement contains a long, less commonly used word when a shorter, more direct word would be acceptable.
- D. The statement contains a colloquial expression that normally is avoided in business writing.

6. The fact that this activity will afford an opportunity to meet your group.   6.____

7. Do you think that the two groups can join together for next month's meeting?   7.____

8. This is one of the most exciting new innovations to be introduced into our college.   8.____

2 (#4)

9. We expect to consummate the agenda before the meeting ends tomorrow at noon.   9._____

10. While this seminar room is small in size, we think we can use it.   10._____

11. Do you think you can make a modification in the date of the Budget Committee meeting?   11._____

12. We are cognizant of the problem but we think we can ameliorate the situation.   12._____

13. Shall I call you around three on the day I arrive in the City?   13._____

14. Until such time that we know precisely that the students will be present.   14._____

15. The consensus of opinion of all the members present is reported in the minutes.   15._____

Questions 16-25.

DIRECTIONS: For each of Questions 16 through 25, select from the options given below the MOST applicable choice.
      A. The sentence is correct.
      B. The sentence contains a spelling error only.
      C. The sentence contains an English grammar error only.
      D. The sentence contains both a spelling error and an English grammar error.

16. Every person in the group is going to do his share.   16._____

17. The man who we selected is new to this University.   17._____

18. She is the older of the four secretaries on the two staffs that are to be combined.   18._____

19. The decision has to be made between him and I.   19._____

20. One of the volunteers are too young for his complicated task, don't you think?   20._____

21. I think your idea is splindid and it will improve this report considerably.   21._____

22. Do you think this is an exagerated account of the behavior you and me observed this morning?   22._____

23. Our supervisor has a clear idea of excelence.   23._____

24. How many occurences were verified by the observers?   24._____

25. We must complete the typing of the draft of the questionaire by noon tomorrow.   25._____

KEY (CORRECT ANSWERS)

1. A
2. C
3. B
4. C
5. A

6. A
7. B
8. B
9. C
10. B

11. C
12. C
13. D
14. A
15. B

16. A
17. C
18. C
19. C
20. D

21. B
22. D
23. B
24. B
25. B

www.ingramcontent.com/pod-product-compliance
Lightning Source LLC
Chambersburg PA
CBHW082149300426
44117CB00016B/2667